AF560761

DALITS IN INDIA

Dalits in India

RELIGION AS A SOURCE OF BONDAGE OR LIBERATION WITH SPECIAL REFERENCE TO CHRISTIANS

JAMES MASSEY

MANOHAR
2026

First published 1995
Reprinted 2024, 2025, 2026

ISBN 978-81-19953-14-1 (Hb)
ISBN 978-81-7304-135-8 (Pb)

Published by
Ajay Kumar Jain for
Manohar Publishers & Distributors
4753/23 Ansari Road, Daryaganj
New Delhi 110 002

Printed and bound in India by Replika Press Pvt. Ltd.

IN MEMORY OF
MY REVERED PARENTS
THE REV. JALAL MASIH
AND
MRS FAZL BIBI
WHO FAITHFULLY SERVED THEIR COMMUNITY
AND HAVE BEEN A CONTINUED SOURCE OF INSPIRATION
TO ME IN MY WORK

Contents

Preface

Dalits in India: Religion as a Source of Bondage or Liberation with Special Reference to Christians is divided into three parts: Dalits and History, Dalit Identity and Basic Rights, and Dalits and Enabling Strategies. Each part comprises two chapters. The material here is based upon research papers written during the period May 1990 – September 1993 for different seminars and consultations. Part of this material has also been published in different journals, such as *Religion and Society* of the Christian Institute for the Study of Religion and Society (CISRS), Bangalore; *Journal of Dharma,* Dharmaram College, Bangalore; *Bulletin of the Christian Institute for Religious Studies*, Baring Union Christian College, Batala, Panjab; and *National Council of Churches Review*, Nagpur. Part of the material in chapter one has also been published under the CISRS's "Dalit Theology Program" as a monograph in 1991. Even though the material has been completely revised and updated, some repetition and an occasional lack of coherence has been unavoidable because of the three year span over which the papers were written and the different audiences they catered to.

This work, in its present form, was submitted to the Johann Wolfgang Goethe-University, Frankfurt am Main, for the Habilitation (Religious Studies) for a post-doctoral award. It would not have been possible without the guidance of Prof. Dr. Edmund Weber and the help of his wife, Mrs Barbara Weber, to whom I am indeed grateful. Special thanks are due to Dr. Lothar Engel, his colleague Rev. Dr. Klaus Schaefer, and Mr. Frank Kurschner of EMW for their encouragement and for providing the much-needed scholarship without which it would not have been possible for me to complete this study.

I am also particularly grateful to the members of ISPCK Executive Committee, through its President, the Most Rev. Dr. Anand Chandu Lal for granting me the permission to undertake this work and motivating me time and again. Among my friends, I would specially like to acknowledge the support which Dr. C.O. McMullen, Rev. R.M. Chaudhary and Dr. Paul Loffler extended me. I must also record my thanks to my colleagues Mr. Asish Amos, Mr. Kalyan Peterson, Mrs. Sadique and the rest of the ISPCK staff for their help and co-operation. I am indebted to my publisher Mr. Ramesh Jain and his son Ajay Jain for their suggestions and keen interest. I am also thankful to my wife Kala and daughters Jyotsna, Kiran and Ujwalla for their constant encouragement all through my study period.

Above all I am grateful to God Almighty for giving me the strength to complete this work.

20 January 1995 JAMES MASSEY

Abbreviations

A.D. :	Anno Domini (in the year of the Lord)
A.P. :	American Presbyterian
ante :	Before
AISCF :	All India Scheduled Castes Federation
B.C. :	Before Christ
BJP :	Bharatiya Jantaa Party
etc. :	Etcetera, and so forth
Enl :	Enlarged
ICHI :	Independent Commission on International Humanitarian Issues
Ibid. :	Ibidem, in the same place
Infra :	Below
MCR :	Mandal Commission Report
NRSV :	New Revised Standard Version
n.d. :	No date
No. :	Numbers
OBC :	Other Backward Classes
Op. cit. :	Opere citato, in the work cited
RPI :	Republican Party of India
SC :	Scheduled Caste
ST :	Scheduled Tribe
S.V. :	Sub verbo, under the word
Vide :	See
Viz. :	Videlicet, Namely
WCC :	World Council of Churches

Introduction

The Subject and Scope

One section of Indian society, which has drawn considerable attention during the last decade of scholars and activists are the people who call themselves 'Dalits' (oppressed).[1] Many works have appeared dealing with their plight, drawing on sources both Christians and others.

Some of these works deal with the history of the Dalit problem and its relationship with the caste system, having its roots in the Hindu religion;[2] some deal with the role of Dalits in politics;[3] some with regional group(s) of Dalits and their struggle to change their status in society;[4] some describe the role played by individual leaders in the struggle of the Dalits;[5] some discuss the question of reservation, known also as compensatory discrimination or preferential treatment of Dalits;[6] some present individual experiences, more like autobiographies;[7] some offer analyses of the Dalit problem either by dealing with the Dalit movement in a particular region or different regions of India or with the question of mobility from one religion to another.[8] Some works have also appeared as anthologies of selections of Dalits' works (in English translation).[9] Some of the works have been reprinted. New ones have also appeared, which are more aggressive from the Dalits' point of view.[10] Recent works deal with the question of people belonging to upper castes and their being indigenous.[11] A number of works, which have come from Christian sources, deal particularly with the history of the Christian Dalits, the question of theology and women.[12] Connected in particular with the Dalits who profess Hinduism, Buddhism and Sikhism and are recognised by the Government of India under the *Presidential Order 1950* (amended in 1956 and 1990) as Scheduled Castes,[13] the most authentic and comprehensive work has been published by the Anthropological

Survey of India. This work gives detailed identification of 450 Dalit communities out of 751. According to the Census 1981, these dalits formed 15.75 per cent of India's poppulation, and numbered 104,754,623.[14] Acording to the Census of India 1991, the number of Dalits belonging to the above three religions is 138,223,277 out of a total population of 846,320,688.[15]

The available works thus deal mostly with specific aspects of the Dalit issue such as the caste system or the aspect of the Dalits' struggle in some regions of India. None of them deals directly with the overall history of the Dalits and the development of their problem. Also, these do not deal with other religions to which large numbers of Dalits have converted, which include Christianity, Islam, Buddhism, Sikhism, Veerasaivism and Baha'i religion. There are other religions in India also, which include Jainism, Judaism and Zoroastrianism, which have been very rarely referred to, when it comes to the the Dalit problem. *David G. Mandelbaum's Society in India* is perhaps the only work which has touched on these religions and tried to show how much these religions could act as agents of social change for the Dalits.[16] But the scope and discussion of Mandelbaum's work is also limited.

The present work studies this subject of religion as a source of bondage or liberation with a special reference to the casteless Christians. It will deal first, with the Dalits in general in India, the history of their problem, and the basic question of their identity. The discussion of their history will also include the role of religion and how far it has acted as an agent of bondage or liberation for the Dalits. The religions which will be referred to in this work are Hinduism, Buddhism, Jainism, Sikhism, Lingayatism (Veerasaivism), Christianity, Islam, Judaism, Zoroastrianism and Baha'i religion.

This work does not deal with all these ten religions in detail. It will discuss in detail the role of Hindu religion, particularly in the historical development of the Dalit problem with special reference to the caste system. In the history of the Dalit problem enough reference will be made to the role of the other nine religions. Reference will be made more in the chronological order than according to their Semitic or orientalistic background.

Besides Hindu religion, detailed references are made to Christian religion or faith with emphasis on Casteless Christians. Christian Dalits are casteless because they belong to a community who in their pre-Dalit state were casteless and classless people.[17] Also Christians are supposed to be casteless, because Christian religion is supposed to be the most egalitarian religion, which means above caste or class.[18]

In chapters one and three, the present work deals with the issue of the Dalits in general. Chapters two and four discuss the special case of the Christian Dalits. Chapter five deals with both, the Dalits in general and the special case of the Christian Dalits, while addressing the whole Indian Christian community or the Church for a response. In Chapter six, the need is underlined for a fresh understanding of Christian faith and its role or a new expression of Indian Christian theology, which possibly will help the Christian community or the Church in India to involve itself more actively in the whole issue of the Dalits, which includes the interests of Christian Dalits.

The Term 'Dalit'

The term *dalit* in Sanskrit is both a noun and an adjective. As a noun, *dalit* may be used for all three genders, masculine, feminine and neuter. It has been derived from the root *dal* which means to crack, open, split, and so on. When used as a noun or adjective, it means burst, split, broken or torn asunder, downtrodden, scattered, crushed, destroyed.[19]

The present usage of the term *dalit* goes back to the nineteenth century when a Marathi social reformer and revolutionary Mahatma Jotirao Phule used it to describe the outcastes and untouchables as the oppressed and broken victims of the Indian caste-ridden society.[20] At the same time it is believed that this usage was first coined by B.R. Ambedkar.[21] But it was during the 1970s that followers of the Dalit Panther Movement of Maharashtra gave currency to the term *Dalit* as a constant reminder of their age-old oppression, denoting both their state of deprivation and people who are oppressed.[22] Today this term is used frequently and has become popular among the Dalit people of various protest movements in India and even in Christian circles.

Besides its common use, the term *dalit* today is specially used for those people who, on the basis of caste distinction, have been considered "outcaste". They were "outcaste", because they were not according to the architects of the system fit to be included in the fourfold graded caste structure of Indian society.[23] On the basis of this status they were made to bear extreme kinds of disabilities in the form of oppression for centuries, which made them almost lose their humanness. In the present work, the term *Dalit* is used to describe these people, many of whom today (as mentioned earlier), prefer to use the term for themselves.This term for them is not a mere name or title; in fact it has become an expression of hope for them in recovering their past identity. Because of these people regarded as outcastes and their struggle, the term *Dalit* has gained a new connotation, which has more positive meaning.[24]

Though the investigation in the present work is based on written sources available, both primary and secondary, some discussion is also based on personal discussion or living experiences with some individuals and places.

A number of technical and Indian terms have been used Their meanings are sometimes given in brackets, but in order not to detract from readability, a glossary of such terms and words is added at the end.

NOTES AND REFERENCES

1. Oommen, T.K.: *Protest and Change, Studies in Social Movements*, New Delhi, 1990, p. 254.
2. (a) Mukherjee, Prabhati: *Beyond the Four Varnas*, Delhi, 1988.

   (b) Rao, R. Sangeetha: *Caste System in India: Myth and Reality*, New Delhi, 1989.

   (c) Ambedkar, B.R.: "Who Were the Shudras? How did they come to be the Fourth Varna in the Indo-Aryan Society", in *Dr. Babasaheb Ambedkar: Writings and Speeches*, Vol. 7, edited by Vasant Moon, Government of Maharashtra, Bombay, 1990. pp. 1-227.

   (d) Ambedkar, B.R.: "The Untouchables, —Who were they and why they became Untouchables", in *ibid*, pp. 228-382.

   (e) Sharma, Ram Sharan: *Sudras in Ancient India*, Delhi,1990 (3rd rev. edn).

(f) Phule, Jotirao Govindrao: "Slavery" *in Collected Works of Mahatma Jotirao Phule,* translated by Prof. P.G. Patil, Government of Maharashtra, Bombay, 1991.

(g) Patil, Sharad, *Dasa-Sudra Slavery*, Pune, 1991.

3. (a) Gupta, S.K.: *The Scheduled Castes in Modern Indian Politics*, New Delhi, 1985.

(b) Chousalkar, Ashok S.: "Social and Political implication of Dalit Movement" in Maharashtra in *Social Reform Movements in India*, V.D. Divekar (ed.), Bombay, 1991.

(c) Gokhale, Jayashree: *From Concessions to Confrontation, The Politics of an Indian Untouchable Community*, Bombay, 1993.

4. (a) Juergensmeyer, Mark: *Religion as Social Vision – The Movement against Untouchability in 20th Century Punjab*, Berkeley, 1982.

(b) Gooptu, Nandini: "Caste, Deprivation and Politics: The Untouchables in U.P. Towns in the Early Twentieth Century", *in Dalit Movements and the Meanings of Labour in India*, Bombay, 1993.

5. (a) O'Hanlon, Rosalind: *Caste, Conflict, and Ideology – Mahatma Jotirao Phule and Low Caste Protest in Nineteenth Century Western India*, Cambridge, 1985.

(b) Zelliot, Eleanor: *From Untouchable to Dalit – Essays on Ambedkar Movement*, New Delhi, 1992.

6. (a) Galanter, Marc: *Competing Equalities, Law and the Backward Classes in India* (see chapter 5 on the designation of the Scheduled Castes and Scheduled Tribes), Bombay, 1984.

(b) Kananaikil, Jose: "The Scheduled Castes and their Status in India", in *Inequalities, its Basis: Search for Solutions,* Walter Fernandes (ed.), New Delhi, 1986, pp. 85-100.

7. (a) Khare, R.S.: *The Untouchable as Himself: Ideology, Identity, and Pragmatism among the Lucknow Chamars,* Cambridge, 1984.

(b) Das, D.P.: *The Untouchable*, New Delhi, 1985.

8. (a) Aggarwal, Partap Chand: *Halfway to Equality*, New Delhi, 1983.

(b) Joshi, Barbara R. (ed.) *Untouchable! Voices of the Dalit Liberation Movement*, New Delhi, 1986.

(c) Murugkar, Lata: *Dalit Panther Movement in Maharashtra*, Bombay, 1991.

9. (a) Anand, Mulk Raj and Eleanor Zelliot (eds), *An Anthology of Dalit Literature (*Poems), New Delhi, 1992.

(b) Dangle, Arjun: *Poisoned Bread* (Translations from Modern Marathi Dalit Literature), New Delhi, 1992.

10. (a) Swami Dharma Theertha: *History of Hindu Imperialism*, Madras, 1992 (5th edn).

(b) Kurundkar, Narhar: *Manusmriti–Contemporary Thoughts*, Bombay, 1993.

11. (a) Elst, Koenraad: *Indigenous Indians – Agastya to Ambedkar*, New Delhi, 1993.

(b) Rajaram, Navaratna S.: *Aryan Invasion of India, The Myth and the Truth*, New Delhi, 1993.
(c) Talageri, Shrikant G.: *Aryan Invasion Theory and Indian Nationalism*, New Delhi, 1993.
(d) Sethna, K.D.: *The Problem of Aryan Origins – From an Indian Point of View, 1992* (second extensively enlarged edition).

12. (a) Prabhakar, M.E. (ed.), *Towards Dalit Theology*, Delhi, 1989.
(b) Irudayaraj, Xavier (ed.), *Emerging Dalit Theology*, Madurai, 1990.
(c) Nirmal, Arvind P., *Heuristic Exploration*, Madras, 1990 (See chapter on "Towards a Christian Dalit Theology," pp. 138-56).
(d) Webster, John C.B., *The Dalit Christians, A History*, Delhi, 1992.
(e) Devasahayaram, V. (ed.), *Dalits and Women*, Madras, 1992.
13. Singh, K.S.: *The Scheduled Castes, People of India, National Series Volume II*, Anthropological Survey of India, Delhi, 1993, p. 2.
14. *Ibid.*, pp. 1, 3.
15. Census of India, 1991, Series 1, India, Paper 1 of 1992, Final Population Totals, New Delhi 1993, p. 15.
16. Mandelbaum, David G.: *Society in India*, Bombay, 1990 (reprinted), pp. 524-72.
17. Wilson, Dr. K.: *The Twice Alienated, Culture of Dalit Christians*, Hyderabad, 1982, p. VI (Introduction).
18. Forrester, Duncan B.: *Caste and Christianity*, London, 1980, pp. 8-10.
19. S.V. *dal* and *dalit*, in *A Sanskrit-English Dictionary* by Sir Monier Monier-Williams, Delhi, 1988 (reprinted), p. 471; and also *The Practical Sanskrit-English Dictionary* by Vaman Shivram Apte, Delhi, 1989 (reprinted), p. 493.
20. Zelliot, Eleanor, *op.cit.*, p.271.
21. Murugkar, Lata, *op.cit.*, p.6.
22. See "Dalit Panthers Manifesto" *in* Joshi, Barbara R. (ed.), *op.cit.*, pp. 141-7.
23. The fourfold caste structure included the Priestly (Brahman), Warrior (Ksatriya), Traders (Vaisya) and Serving caste (Sudras).
24. See Joshi, Barbara R. (ed.), *op.cit.*, p. 3.

PART I

Dalits and History

CHAPTER ONE

Historical Roots of the Dalits

Introduction

In this chapter an attempt is made to reach the roots of the Dalits, but this is a difficult task, because nothing has been left in written form by their forebearers. All that is available in writing is what is left mostly by their rivals, which of course, cannot be taken as direct evidence or material for reconstructing the history of the Dalits. But only historical roots can provide the clue to the lost identity of the Dalits; they can also help in answering a number of other pertinent questions: Who are these Dalits? What place do they belong to? How has the present state of the Dalits been created? Who is responsible for it? There are a number of other questions which can be raised concerning the Dalits. There is also a dangerous tendency to regard such questions as being of an academic nature or superfluous, and therefore not relevant. But that is wrong, because these questions and answers to them provide the basis for the various Dalit movements which are working to deal with their problem.

An attempt is made here to make use of as many sources as available within a limited space, time and effort, and to reconstruct the history of the Dalits. If some gaps are still left it will be mainly due to the limitations of availability of literature.

This chapter does not present a comprehensive case of the Dalits, but it may be enough for the purpose of the present study to see the role of religion in the development of the Dalits' problem.

Historical Story

Though in the absence of the right material, it is difficult to write a Dalit history, there are some archaeological and literary sources which lead to the possible historical roots of the Dalits. But the right approach is necessary because material was never prepared for such a purpose. One has to pick the right information from the scattered facts and also read between the lines from the literary sources available. Putting these sources together, one can possibly reconstruct the possible roots of the Dalits.

Where the question of archaeological and literary sources is concerned, it seems the story of the origins of the Dalits goes far back in history. The people known as the Dalits today had definitely a beginning, similar to the beginning of other human beings on earth, but this work is not concerned with that beginning. The concern here is with the moment in history when today's Dalits began their present life as degraded human beings. The archaeological sources which are being referred to are the findings of the excavations which have taken place since A.D. 1920 at various sites in Greater Panjab, part of which now is in Pakistan, and other parts in India. The most famous sites of these excavations are known as Mohenjodaro and Harappa. Between 1920 and 1951, at Mohenjodaro alone three foundations, one upon the other, were unearthed. But the archaeologists have still not reached a possible virgin land upon which the first foundation was laid. They have named these three foundations Mohenjodaro I, Mohenjodaro II and Mohenjodaro III. These three foundations indicate that Mohenjodaro had been destroyed more than once. Along with other related areas excavated, this is known as the Indus Valley Civilisation. Archaeologists have fixed the period of I to III at about 1500 years. The date of the last foundation, Mohenjodaro III has been fixed around 1500 B.C.[1] Interestingly, among the literary sources referred to in this work, the earliest best known is the *Rigveda*. The dates of the composition of the *Rigveda's* hymns also have been put by a number of well known historians between 1500-1000 B.C.[2]

Scholars dealing with the two mentioned sources, archaeological and literary, while fixing the historical relationship of both have not reached a common conclusion. The main question which they have faced is who were the people who formed the Mohenjodaro and Harappan civilisation? Who defeated the dwellers of this ancient civilisation, as a result of which it was destroyed? Though it is difficult to deal with such perplexing questions in one chapter, in order to deal with 'the roots of the Dalits', it is necessary to include these questions in the discussion. Before going into this discussion, it may be good to list the major agreements and disagreements, which scholars have on these questions.

On two points most of the scholars are agreed; and on two other points they have disagreements. These are as follows:

Agreements

(a) Destruction of the Indus Valley Civilisation and contents of the hymns of the *Rigveda* are related. Both these sources point towards a war-conflict among different groups of people (Srivastava, Kapur Singh, Ambedkar, Smith, Basham, Chattopadhyaya, Chanda, D.D. Kosambi, and others).[3] This has a direct relationship with the history of Dalits, because the time of war-conflict of these opposing groups will be the beginnings of the history of the Dalits.

(b) Most of the scholars also agree that the present condition of the Dalits is the result of the long process of our country's history through which they have been reduced to their present state of sub-human' or 'no-people' (Dalit state) existence of misery and poverty (Mukherjee, Srivastava, Ghurye, Dutt, Bhattacharyya and others).[4]

Disagreements

(a) Whether the home of the people known as Aryans is India or outside. Those who believe in the indigenous origin of the Aryans include: Ambedkar, Rao, Koenraad Elst, Navaratna S. Rajaram, Shrikant G. Talageri and K.D. Sethna, among others.[5] The number of scholars who believe that the Aryans came from outside is much larger. They includes: Jyotirao Phule, Ghose, Srivastava, Chanda, Chattopadhyaya, Fuchs, Hutton, Swami Dharma Theertha, Suniti

Kumar Chatterji, Jawaharlal Nehru, D.D. Kosambi, Hermann Kulke and Dietmar Rothermund, among others.[6]

(b) Connected with this point of disagreement, Ambedkar also holds the view that there is no racial difference between the Hindus and the Untouchables.[7] Sangeetha Rao in her work on the caste system in India confirms the views of Ambedkar.[8] In his work N.N. Bhattacharyya also holds views similar to those of Ambedkar that the basis of our ancient society is the tribal system, from which the present Indian society developed.[9]

It will not be possible to deal with all the issues raised by different scholars, but certainly references can be made to the main points. The most important task is to identify the time or period when the Dalits of today started losing their identity. For at that particular time, the history of the Dalits began. Before, they were not in a Dalit state; they were normal human beings enjoying their full self-identity. Therefore, the main concern in the ensuing discussion will be to establish the historical roots of the Dalits. Since the purpose here is not be to discuss the Aryans' origin or homeland, instead of depending on the secondary sources or the conflicting views of different scholars, the two primary sources, namely the *Rigveda* and the findings of the archaeologists will be discussed. The 'historical story' will thus be dealt with under the following heads:

1. The *Rigveda*
2. The Archaeologists
3. The *Rigveda* and the Archaeologists
4. Development of the Dalit problem

Next, the question 'Are Dalits an indigenous people?' will be examined, with brief concluding remarks.

The Rigveda

The *Rigveda* is the earliest written literary source of the ancient history of India. A large part of the text is addressed to Lord Indra, which narrates a fierce war-encounter having taking taken place among different groups. Two opposing forces may be seen in the *Rigveda* – *first*, on whose behalf the hymns of the *Rigveda* are addressed to different gods and, *second*, against whom they are addressed. Ramprasad Chanda has made this important observation: "These hymns reveal two hostile peoples in the land of the Seven Rivers now called the Panjab – the deva worshipping Arya and deva-less and the riteless Dasyu or Dasa."[10] To know more about these two opposing groups, a few of the relevant verses from the hymns of the *Rigveda* are examined below. These verses are listed in seven sets and then brief comments are offered on them:

I. (a) *vi janihayaran ye ch dasyvo. . .*[11]
You (Indra) know well Aryas and Dasyus. . .
(b) *. . .hatavi dusyun prarya vaarnamavata.*[12]
. . .he (Indra) killed the Dasyus and protected the Aryan race (colour).

II. (a) *Indra panch Kachhatinama.*[13]
Indra is the ruler of the five (races).
(b) *Tadindragni Yadus Turvasesu yad*
Druhyus Pavanusu Purusus sath.[14]
O Indra-Agni, you live among (the people of)
the Yadus, Turvasas, Druhyus, Anus and Purus.
(c) *par yat samudramati sur parshi*
paraya Turvasa Yadu svasita.[15]
O hero (Indra)! When you came over the sea,
you brought over it Turvasa and Yadu.

III. (a) vadhihi *dasyu dhanini. . .*[16]
You (Indra) killed rich Dasyu. . .
(b) *akarma dasyurabhi no amanturanya-varto amanus.*[17]
All around us are ritualless Dasyu, inhuman,
who are following alien laws.
(c) *anaso dasyu. . .*[18]
Noseless dasyu. . .

IV. (a) *sa jatubharma chhadadadhana ojo.*
puro vimindannacharada vi dasi.
vidana vajirna dasyuve hetimasnarya
saho vadhrya sumnamindar. . .
dasyu hatyaya.[19]
Armed with his thunderbolt, Indra went about
destroying the forts of Dasas.

O Indra, throw your thunderbolt at the Dasyus,
increase the power and glory of Aryas.

(b) *yo hatavahimarinata sapat sindhuna*
yo ga udajadapadha valasaya,
yo asamanorantargina jajana
savivak sa janam Indra.[20]
One who killed the Dragon and freed the Seven Rivers (*Sapatsindhu*):
he who drove the cows from the Vala,
One who created fire between stones,
and had beaten the warriors in the battle.
He, O people, is Indra.

(c) *sa vartrahendra Karsunayoni*
purandaro dasiraraiyada vi. . .
hatavi dasyuna pura ayasinin tarita.[21]
Indra the Vartra-killer, fort-destroyer,
scattered the dasa,
who dwelt in darkness. . .
he killed the Dasyus
and broke the forts made of iron.

V. (a) *dasa cha vartra hatamayrani cha*
Sudasmindravrunavasavatama.[22]
Indra and Varuna killed the Dasa and Arya
who were Sudas' enemies and helped him with favour.

(b) *yo no dasa ayro vapurustutadeva*
Indra yudhve chiketati.[23]
O Most respected Indra, the godless people,
whether Dasas or Arya, who want war with us.

VI. (a) *yatha deva asureshu sadramugaresu chakirre.*[24]
Even the gods kept faith in the mighty Asuras.

(b) *hatyaya deva asurana. . .*[25]
When the gods killed Asuras. . .

VII (a) *apasedhana raksaso yatudhanansthada deva:. . .*[26]
Driving off raksasas and Yatudhanas, the god is present. . .

(b) *jahi nyatrina pani varko hisa*[27]
You (Soma) kill Pani. He is like a wolf.

The main point of the first set of two verses of hymn 51 of Mandala book one, and hymn 34 of Mandala three is that the *Rigveda* definitely deals with two different groups of people. These are *the Aryas* and *the Dasyus*. *The Aryas* in hymn 3.34.9 are addressed as *varna* (races). According to the authors of the *Vedic Index of Names and Subjects,* "Arya is the normal designation in Vedic literature from the *Rigveda* onwards of an Aryan, a member of the three upper classes: Brahman, Ksatriya, or Vaisya...the Arya stands in opposition to the Dasa, but also to the Sudra."[28] Regarding the Dasyu, the authors of the *Vedic Index* on the basis of some passages of the *Rigveda* (1.51.8, 103.3; 2.18.19; 3.34.9 etc.) see the possibility of their being indigenous people, who are addressed in the *Rigveda* with special negative traits, which are nowhere applied in the same text to Aryas. The Dasyu according to the *Rigveda* are: *anas* (without face), *anaso* (noseless), etc.[29] The distinction between the Aryas and the Dasyu is affirmed by V.S. Apte also.[30]

The second set of verses 1.7.9, 1.108.8 and 6.20.2 make a few important points about Aryas. Verse 1.7.9 makes the point that Indra was the ruler of the five races. Who are these five races (*panch*)? A number of views are offered to answer this question.[31] Two main views are that *panch* here refers to the four *varna* (castes) and the fifth indigenous group known as *Nisadas*. According to the second view, the *panch* here refers to the five main tribes of Arya people, *Yadu, Turvasa, Druhyu, Anu* and *Puru*. On the basis of the various testimonies available from the text of other hymns of the *Rigveda*, particularly the hymn from the second verse of the second set quoted 1.108.8, the second view can be supported more easily that *panch* here refers to the Aryas' five main tribes. Also when the hymns of the *Rigveda* such as 1.7.9 were composed such a caste distinction did not exist.[32] The third verse, 6.20.2 of this set, hints at the Arya people coming across the sea, if the term *samudra* is taken to be the sea. Ramprasad Chanda strongly supports this possibility and says:

> According to some scholars *samudra* in the Rigveda does not mean sea, for the Aryas had not yet reached the sea, but only the lower course of the Indus. This interpretation of *samudra*

> may be traced to the preconceived notion that the Rigveda Aryas were a homogeneous body of men who came from the north-west. But once this notion is dismissed from the mind, there is nothing left to prevent us from accepting *samudra* in its usual sense. The sea that lies the nearest to the country of the *Rigveda* Aryas is the Arabian Sea. So if we are to attach any value to this Vedic tradition, we are forced to assume that the Yadus and the Turasas came across the Arabian Sea. The evidences contained in the later Vedic and Epic literature relating to the Indian home of one of these two folks, the Yadus, lend support to this hypothesis.[33]

The third set of verses 1.38.4, 10.22.8 and 5.38.10 list some examples of allusions to the Dasyus in the *Rigveda*; they also highlight some traits of the Dasyus, which separate them from the Aryas both racially and culturally. A number of hymns of the *Rigveda* tell that the Dasyus were rich and well to do (10.22.8); they also lived in well-fortified houses and cities.[34] They are also contemptuously said to be ritualless, inhuman, following alien laws (verse 10.22.38). The Dasyus had their own religious and social customs and rites, which were alien to the Aryas but not to them. The Dasyus are also described as "noseless" (verse 5.38.10), which means the appearance of their faces differed from that of Aryas. In other hymns of the *Rigveda* their colour is described as dark with dusky skin.[35]

The verses in set four and other references in the *Rigveda* describe how under the command of Lord Indra, the Aryas defeated, destroyed, scattered and looted the Dasyus or Dasas. A large part of the *Rigveda* glorifies Lord Indra for his capacity for war as against his and the Aryas' enemy (*sataru*). Thus, Indra fought with the Dasas (Dasyus) and destroyed their forts (verse 1.103.4, 4). Indra's war efforts increased the power and glory of the Aryas. Hymn 2.12.3 refers (it seems) to one of the main victories of Lord Indra, in which he killed his chief enemy (*Sapat* which means Dragon) and freed (the land of) seven rivers (*Sapat-Sindhu*), which means the land from river Sindh to Sarasvati (almost the whole of North India, part of which is now in Pakistan and part in the present North India).

In hymn 2.20.7,8 again Lord Indra is shown as the killer of *vartra* (a common name used in the *Rigveda* for Indra's powerful enemies), destroyer of forts, killer of the Dasyus (or the Dasas) and also scattering them all over. In hymn 2.12.4 Indra is further shown chasing, defeating, and looting his enemy's riches. In 7.5.3 the author describes how the dark-skinned races fled, scattered abroad and left behind their possessions.

The two verses in set five (78.3.1 and 10.38.3) bring to light new information about the war affairs of Lord Indra. Here he is shown fighting both with his Dasa and Aryan enemies (7.83.1). On the basis of such verses some scholars, particularly Ambedkar, have tried to work out a theory that both the opposing forces in these verses are Aryan.[36] How he has arrived at this conclusion is not clear; neither has he offered incontrovertible evidence to prove his thesis. The *Rigveda* itself offers clear assistance in the matter. For example, hymn 18 of Mandala 7 of the *Rigveda* narrates a major event, the battle of ten tribes. In this war, ten tribes were on one side, that is, *Puru, Yadu, Turvasa, Anu* and *Drahyu* assisted by five smaller tribes *Alina, Pakthas Bhalana, Siva* and *Visanin.*

It is seen from verses listed in set two that the first five tribes were Aryan. The five other smaller tribes – *Paktha, Bhalana, Alina, Siva* and *Visanin,* it seems, were non-Aryan. Griffith has labelled all the ten tribes as "the non-Aryan confederacy".[37] K.P. Chattopadhyaya's observations on this issue are also notable. According to him:

> The *Rigveda* tribes were not homogeneous. It has been pointed out by Vedic scholars that the battle of ten kings mentioned in the *Rigveda* was probably between two groups who differed in language. The Purus who led the ten tribes were called *mrdhvavacan,* i.e. speakers of incorrect or corrupt speech (*Rigveda* VII 18-13). Their opponents the Bharatas under Sudas were speakers of correct speech . . . the leadership of the antagonists of Sudas and the Bharatas was, therefore, partly of Asura descent . . . This Asura character of the Purus would explain their speakers of a somewhat different speech.[38]

These observations and the above quoted verses from the *Rigveda* help in understanding the complexity of Indra fighting both his Dasa and Arya enemies, but certainly they are not the same, though there is a real possibility of the existence of mixed racial groups, particularly during the later Vedic period.

The last two sets of verses indicate the existence of other non-Aryan people with whom also the Aryans waged war. These included the Asuras (10.151.3; 10.157.4), the Raksasas (1.35.10) and the Pani (6.51.14).

The Archaeologists

Archaeological sources are a great help in reaching the historical roots of the Dalits. Archeological literature, certainly, has not been written keeping the Dalits in mind but it throws much light on the ancient people of India. The *Ancient Cities of the Indus*[39] edited by Gregory L. Possehl is a superb work of reference, for our purpose. It includes the main research papers written between 1924 and 1979 and contains, among others, the works of the famous pioneer archaeologists John Marshall, Ernest Mackay, Mortimer Wheeler, and the well-known Indian archaeologists S.R. Rao, Gurdip Singh, C. Ramasamy, Iravatham Mahadevan and B.M. Pandey. The other works referred to are the *Early Indus Civilization* by Ernest Mackay[40] and *The Indus Civilization* by Mortimer Wheeler.[41] Given below are brief relevant extracts from the works of various authorities in the field of archaeology on the nature of the Indus Valley Civilisation. Four aspects are covered, namely (a) that it was a well-established civilisation, (b) the nature of the people, (c) the date of the civilisation, and (d) how it met with its end.

1. *Well-established Civilization*

(a) In the field of exploration, it is natural this year to give the premier place to the remarkable discoveries made by the Department in Sindh and the South West Panjab . . . Hitherto India has almost universally been regarded as one of the younger countries of the world... Now, at a single bound, we have taken back our knowledge of

Indian civilization some 3000 years earlier and have established the fact that in the 3rd millennium before Christ and even before that the people of Panjab and Sind were living in well-built cities and were in possession of a relatively mature culture with a high standard of art and craftsmanship and developed a system of pictorial writing. The sites where these discoveries have been made are at Harappa in the Montgomery District of the Panjab and Mohenjodaro, more than 400 miles away, in the Larkana District of Sindh.[42] —*John Marshall, 1923-24*

(b) The Indus Valley Culture, or Harappa culture as it is called after the name of the village occupying the site . . . The known remains of this culture, with all its ramifications, occupy a broad triangular area in North-West India and West Pakistan, extending from the foot of the Himalayas to the Makram Coast, Gujarat, Bahawalpur and North-Western Rajasthan, covering nearly 1000 miles from Sutkagu Dor near the foot of Sivaliks in the extreme north-west. Further explorations have now pushed the limit of this culture from Cambay in the south of the Jamuna Basin, about 30 miles north of Delhi. The Harappa culture is essentially a riverine culture . . .[43]

—*Gurdip Singh, 1971*

(c) It does suggest that the Indus Valley Civilization was an indigenous development that arose out of the evolution of developed village cultures in a favourable environment. It emphasizes the sub-continental roots and the consequent "style" which gives the civilization its uniqueness.[44]

—*Walter A. Fairservis. Jr., 1967*

II. *The People*

(a) Who were these people who built Mohenjodaro and Harappa? No definite answer can be given at present to this question, though it is certain that they were a pre-Aryan race, for their cities were flourishing some thousand years before any Aryan-speaking people had entered India, which took place, according to modern ruling, about 1500 B.C.[45] —*Ernest Mackay, 1935*

(b) If, as seems likely, it is permissible to take the costume worn by the clay figurines of the Mother Goddess as representative of the normal attire of the feminine population of Mohenjodaro and Harappa ... as nearly the same costume is worn by many of the women of Southern India, the view may provisionally be accepted that the dress of the figurines was the usual feminine attire of the Harappa period, especially as there is strong reason to believe that the climate of north-west India has altered considerably since the middle of the third millennium B.C.[46] —*Ernest Mackay, 1935*

(c) Without identifying the symmetry of the people with any particular racial stock, the late Dr. Guha had said that the skulls from stratum II belonged to a large-headed dolicocephalic type with well-developed supra-orbital ridges and high cranial roof, long face and prominent nose. These features, according to him, showed a continuity of the Indus people of Harappa and Mohenjodaro. However, in the pot burials of Stratum I, Guha had observed an element of small, low-headed people, and this, Vats thought, indicated "a definite admixture" which might be due to racial or cultural upheaval brought about by the immigration of a foreign people into this district of the Panjab.[47] —*H.D. Sankalia, 1972-73*

(d) There is now incontrovertible archaeological evidence that the major population shift was to the south-east into the area of the Kathiawar peninsula north of Bombay. Here the Harappans mingled with other indigenous populations and gradually there was complete absorption and transformation of the remnants of the formerly great Harappan culture into what we are coming to recognize as a distinctive chalcolithic culture of Central India.[48]

—*George F. Dales, 1964*

III. *Date*

(a) Thus of the twelve seals for which any sort of dating can be postulated, seven may be Sargonid, one pre-Sargonid and four of the Larsa or later periods. On current dating, the maximum period required to cover these possibilities would be 2500-1500 B.C., with a strong focus on 2550 B.C.[49] —*Mortimer Wheeler, 1953*

(b) Now that general archaeological opinion is in favour of dating the uppermost levels of Mohenjodaro to the seventeenth century...[50] —*Ernest Mackay, 1935*

IV. *End*

(a) In the course of excavations at Mohenjodaro in 1925-26, several groups of skeletons were found... Excavation elsewhere in the city has laid bare other groups of skeletons, one being of special interest. In this group the remains of some members of the party lay at the foot of a staircase leading down from a street to a well, while one, a woman, had nearly climbed up to the level of the street, but had succumbed on the top step (P1.1,2). It was thought at first that an epidemic disease must have been responsible for these deaths, but this theory was refuted by the later discovery of two more groups... It now seems certain that Mohenjodaro was attacked by enemies during, at least one period of its later history... The subsidence of walls and well-livings at two distinct levels of the city, one much lower than the other, proves that it was flooded early in the history of Mohenjodaro and that another marked the beginning of its decline.[51] —*Ernest Mackay, 1935*

(b) Tentatively, the evidence suggests that Mohenjodaro and much of the lower Indus Valley suffered from a series of severe and extensive floods which eventually forced most of the population to abandon the area, possibly around 1800 or 1700 B.C.[52] —*George F. Dales, 1966*

Among the four sets of extracts from the works of various authorities on the archaeological findings on Mohenjodaro and Harappa, the first set establishes that there was a well established civilisation in our country even before 3,000 years. John Marshall's findings quoted above are still the best possible summary of the description of this ancient civilization. His comment is notable where he writes, "In the 3rd millennium B.C. and even before that, the people of the Panjab and Sindh were living in well-built cities and were in possession of a relatively mature culture with a high standard of art and craftsmanship and a developed system of pictorial writing." John Marshall's contention has been supported by a number of other authorities.[53] Samuel N. Kramer in his essay "The Indus Civilization and Dilmun: The Sumerian Paradise Land" says:

> To be sure the Indus people did have a well-developed system of writing consisting of some four hundred pictorial signs... One of the most striking and impressive features of the Indus cities and towns... water and cleanliness seem to have played an important role in the life of people, as is evident from the extraordinary number of wells and baths in both public and private buildings, as well as the carefully planned network of covered drains built of kiln-baked bricks.[54]

The second point from the first set of extracts is that the Indus Valley culture was basically a "riverine culture" which covered the whole of old Panjab, starting almost from Iran's border and spreading beyond Delhi. These two points are confirmed by Gurdip Singh in his essay on "The Indus Valley Culture" in the second passage of set one quoted above. It is also confirmed by Mortimer Wheeler in his work *The Indus Civilization.* He even said, "For what such claims are worth, the Indus Civilization can thus claim a larger area than any other of the known pre-classical civilizations."[55]

The third point is that "the Indus Valley civilisation was an indigenous development" and it had its roots in the Indian subcontinent itself.

The second set of extracts on "people" makes a number of important points with regard to the kind of people who were living in the various ancient cities and towns of the Indus. They were pre-Aryan (extract 'a'); resemblance to these pre-Aryan people is still found in India, particularly in the southern India (extract 'b'). The clothes which small idols of a female goddess wear include a small *dhoti* (half sari, which goes from the waist to the knee only). This kind of clothes and similar style of hair of these female idols are still found in some parts of the western coast of Tamil Nadu. There is further support to this truth from the fact that during the middle of the third millennium the climate of north-west India was the same as is common to the western coast of Tamil Nadu; and because of the warm climate, heavy clothing was not needed.[56]

The third extract adds a further element about the possible race of people who were living at the site of Mohenjodaro or Harappa. Though Ernest Mackay is clear that they were pre-Aryan, H.D. Sankalia points out a possible racial admixture, because of the immigration of a foreign people into the Panjab of that time. But before H.D. Sankalia, Mortimer Wheeler had made more detailed observations on the issue of people. Besides the skeleton found in a grave at Harappa, he has considered the skeletal remains of people who were massacred in the streets of Mohenjodaro. He has identified four racial groups including the proto-Australoids,who according to him were: "...a small folk with long, narrow skulls, a somewhat broad nose... These features are at home in India, and Ceylon.... In modern language, these folk may be classed as the 'aboriginal' element in the population."[57] Wheeler also means to say that there was one race already living in these ancient cities. What needs to be remembered is that most of these archaeological findings belong to the upper layers, because still archaeologists have not arrived at virgin soil and one does not know how many more layers they will find.[58] The last extract from George F. Dales' essay talks about the movement of Harappa's people towards the south-east and also how these migrated people influenced the culture of Central India. The idea of mixed population also gets support from this extract.

The third set of extracts deals with the date of the Indus Valley Civilisation. On this issue all the leading archaeologists agree more or less, that well civilised people were living in the cities of Harappa and Mohenjodaro before 1500 B.C.[59] Wheeler has tried to fix the period of these people on the basis of twelve seals which were found during the excavations, and has concluded that it should be around 2500-1500 B.C. But these dates only refer to the time when these seals were made; they cannot help us about the exact time of the beginning or how far back the roots of the Indus Valley Civilisation go. Archaeologists have not yet unearth-ed the lowest level upon which the first foundations of the cities were laid.[60] Therefore, Ernest Mackay rightly talks about the date of the uppermost levels of Mohenjodaro being the seventeenth century B.C. On the basis of some evidence found outside India, he has also suggested shifting the date of the end of the Harappa cities into the sixteenth century B.C.[61] Taking into account the views of these well-known archaeologists, one may safely say that the people who were part of the Indus Valley Civilisation were living in the cities of the Indus prior to 1500 B.C.

As far as the date of the destruction of the cities of the Indus is concerned, it is more or less settled above. But the other vital question regarding the Indus Valley Civilisation or destruction of its cities and the cause of this destruction are still to be considered. There are three different theories about this issue put forward by experts. One traditional and more popular theory is the invasion theory, based on the position of some skeletons found during the excavations at Mohenjodaro (see the first extract of group IV above).[62] The second theory, put forward more recently, is that this destruction was due to a series of severe and extensive floods (see extract second of group IV above). There is not much support to this theory.[63] A middle path theory put forward by an archaeologist like Gurdip Singh is:

> The extinction of the Indus culture may have thus been initiated through gradual decline as a result of climatic change, but the process may yet have been completed by successive invasions, from the North-West by the Aryans.[64]

Gurdip Singh expressed this view in 1971. A similar view had been put forward earlier in 1961 by A. Fairservis, Jr.[65]

The third extract of group IV is closer to the first view, only it adds a new insight to the possibility of the destruction of Harappa by Aryan invasion. Even this view sees the influence of the flood factor in the destruction of Indus cities. It seems the middle path theory expressed by Gurdip Singh is closer to probability.

The Rigveda and the Archaeologists

A number of attempts have been made to correlate the information based upon the *Rigveda* and the archaeological works. These attempts have been made by historians like N.N. Bhattacharyya;[66] authorities on the Vedic Age or the Prehistoric Age, which include H.D. Sankalia, S.K. Chatterji, A.D. Pusalkar[67] and K.P. Chattopadhyaya;[68] and a number of other archaeologists such as Mortimer Wheeler[69] and Arlene R.K. Zide.[70] Historians and archeologists have been able to fix the dates only approximately. N.N. Bhattacharyya in his work on *Ancient Indian History and Civilization* has rejected Wheeler's view that the Aryans first destroyed the Harappans, and then erected their own settlement on the same site. On that basis later scholars have fixed the date of Harappa civilisation as 1750 B.C., not 1500 B.C.[71] But then B.K. Ghosh in his essay on "The Aryan Problem" in *The Vedic Age* rightly pointed out that on the basis of the language of the *Rigveda,* an approximate date of its composition can be fixed around 1000 B.C. He adds that the culture it represents can be older and can be pushed up to 1500 B.C. He also confirms that the Mohenjodaro culture is of about 2500 B.C. and possibly that is the time when the first invasion of Aryans took place. The discussion above on dates also points towards such a possibility. Therefore, where the period and date are concerned one may more or less agree with Zide's view:

> The chronology of the Indo-Aryan civilization in India on the other hand, has as its upper limit the date 1200 B.C., but recent examination of the literary evidence of the *Rigveda* and the *Atharva Veda* would place the limit as more probably around 1100 B.C. or even 1000 B.C. The archaeological evidences as well point to such a conclusion, and to a definite break between the Indus Valley civilization and the advent of the Aryan invaders.[72]

The second point is that both the literary (*Rigveda*) and the archaeological sources deal with two groups of people. On one hand, there is an already settled group; on the other hand is an intruder or invaders' group and the violence which took place between these groups (see sections on the *Rigveda* and the Archaeologists). The *Rigveda* names these people as the Aryans and the Dasyu or the Dasas. There are other names of the Aryan tribes as well as of the non-Aryan tribes. The Aryan enemies are also addressed as Asura, Raksasa, Pani etc. Archaeologists, particularly Mortimer Wheeler, have also identified four different groups of people (mention has been made earlier) and one of them is very close to the Dasa or the Dasyus with narrow skulls, and broad nose, (whom the *Rigveda* alluded to as "without face", "noseless", etc.).

Wheeler has even tried to establish a direct relationship with the cities of the Indus civilization and the names of places found in the *Rigveda*. For example, the Rigvedic name Hari-Yupuya, he sees as today's name for Harappa, where he argues, possibly Vrcivants was defeated by Abyavartin Cayamana. The Vrcivants tribe, according to him, "may be connected with Varcin, who was a foe of Indra and, therefore, non-Aryan."[73] Wheeler has also discussed, in detail, the discovery of fortified citadels at Harappa and Mohenjodaro, and forts and citadels mentioned in the *Rigveda* as being destroyed by Indra. According to him these citadels are the same, because the period and dates of their destruction are the same.[74] A.D. Pusalkar discusses in detail the people of the Indus Civilisation and the Rigvedic people.[75] K.P. Chattopadhyaya too has identified the people of Mohenjodaro and Harappa with the Asuras of the *Rigveda*.[76]

Once the identity of the people of the Rigveda and the Indus Civilisation has been agreed upon, other questions related to the destruction and uprooting of different groups of people are easily dealt with. But first, in the light of the discussion above, we may conclude as follows:

(a) The groups of people mentioned in the *Rigveda* are the same as those established by the archaeological findings at places like Mohenjodaro and Harappa. Basically they belonged to two groups, one already settled at these places and the other invaders.

(b) Both the *Rigveda* and the archaeological findings testify to the fact that calamity struck the people and their cities in the form of floods, climatic changes, and in a major way, invasions.

(c) The conflict between the two major groups of people took place around the middle of the second millennium (1500 B.C.). This possibly is the point or moment in history from which the history of the people known as Dalits begins. How the history of the Dalit problem developed from this moment is briefly discussed below.

Historical Development of the Dalit Problem

This section is divided into two parts: the first deals with the early growth of the Dalit problem; and the second, with the period beginning with the period A.D. 700.

Early Development

It should be clear from the discussion above that the history of the Dalits began almost 3,500 years ago. H.G. Wells tells how at that point of history, one group (the nomad folk) defeated the other groups (the settled folk) and how as a result the history of both the groups was completely changed. He wrote:

> Down pour the united nomads on the unwarlike unarmed plains; there ensues a war of conquest. Instead of carrying off the booty, the conquerors settle down on the conquered land which becomes all booty for them; the villagers and townsmen are reduced to servitude and tribute-paying, they become hewers of wood and drawers of water, and the leaders of the nomads become kings and princes, masters and aristocrats.[77]

A number of other writers have also made the same point.[78] The Dalits have been reduced to their present state "by centuries of exploitation and servility".[79] This is corroborated, besides, the *Rigveda,* by other later literary sources. A few references are given below to show this development.

In the *Rigveda*, which is supposed to be the oldest literary source available to us, the famous *Purusasukta* hymn mentions the existence of four castes when it says: "The Brahman was his mouth, of both his arms was the Rajanya (Ksatriya) made, His thighs became the Vaishya, from his feet the Sudra was produced."[80]

On the basis of this hymn, orthodox people believe that the fourfold division of Indian society exists from the earliest times; but according to some scholars, this hymn was composed at a later time and therefore, does not represent the state of the Rigvedic period.[81] This may be true, but it is also true that the Dalit problem took root right in the Rigvedic times as a result of the conflict between two hostile peoples.

The text of *Rigveda* pre-dates 1000 B.C., which is followed by Upanishadic period, which begins around 800 B.C. and closes towards the end of the sixth century B.C.[82] There are references and testimony in the text of the *Upanishads* that by the time these texts came into existence, the problem of the Dalits was getting entrenched. For example, the *Chandogya Upanishad,* not only refers to the three upper castes, but also compares Chandala (outcaste) with a dog or a swine. In the tenth *khanda,* verse seven reads as follows:

> Accordingly, those who are of pleasant conduct here – the prospect is, indeed, that they will enter a pleasant womb, either the womb of a Brahman, or the womb of a Ksatriya, or the womb of a Vaisya. But those who are of stinking conduct here – the prospect is, indeed, that they will enter a stinking womb – either the womb of a dog, or the womb of a swine or the womb of an outcaste (*chandala*).[83]

This verse testifies not only to the existence of caste but also, in the way an outcaste is compared to a dog or a swine or the manner in which the "womb" of the upper caste is addressed as "a pleasant" one and the womb of an outcaste as "a stinking" one, to the further degradation of the Dalits. It also makes clear that from now onwards the caste status also depends upon one's conduct in one's previous birth.

The two great epics, *Ramayana* and *Mahabharata,* explicitly tell us how far the condition of the Dalits had deteriorated by the time these were composed. The period of composition of the *Ramayana* scholars have fixed around fifth century B.C.[84] The period of *Mahabharata* too, scholars have prescribed according to different stages.

Leaving out the early stage, the second and the third stage, the stage with which this discussion is concerned is the stage of the Pandu heroes and of the divine hero Krishna. The period of Pandu stage is between 600 B.C. and 200 B.C. and the Krishna stage 200 B.C. to A.D. 500.[85]

Valmiki, in his text of the *Ramayana* tells through a story, how much the Sudras, the fourth caste, had become degraded (not to speak of the Dalit or outcaste). According to this story, in Lord Rama's time only the three upper castes were allowed to do *tapasya* (penance and meditation). Yet a Sudra undertook penance in order to attain divinity, as a result of which, a Brahman boy of 15 years died. The bereaved father complained to Lord Rama, who after learning of the cause of the death, went in search of the Sudra. On meeting him, Lord Rama said to him:

> You are indeed blessed. Tell me in which caste you have been born. I am Rama, son of Dasaratha. Out of curiosity I have asked you this question. Tell me the truth. Are you a Brahman, Ksatriya or a Sudra?
>
> The ascetic replied, "O King! I am born of Sudra caste. I want to attain divinity by such penance. When I want to attain divinity, I won't tell lies. I am a Sudra by caste, and my name is Samvuka."
>
> As soon as the ascetic uttered those words, Rama drew forth his sword and severed Samvuka's head.[86]

In the continuing narrative it is said that Lord Rama asked the gods to restore the Brahman boy to life and he was told that he had already been revived the moment the Sudra ascetic was killed.

In the *Mahabharata* also there is a reference to the degraded state of the Dalits. The story of Ekalavya, an indigenous boy, tells how he had to lose his right thumb because he had learned archery and was in no way inferior to Arjuna in his skill. Again the main point of the story is how at the time of the *Mahabharata* low castes or the Dalits did not have the right to education.[87]

Srimad Bhagavad Gita also not only affirms faith in the four castes (*chaturvarnyam*), but also tells that these had been created by Lord Krishna himself.[88] It also advises members of each caste to follow faithfully the duties prescribed for them on the basis of their caste.[89] The only difference one finds in the *Bhagavad Gita* is that by taking refuge in Lord Krishna, the outcastes, women, Vaisyas and also Sudras can attain the highest goal.[90]

Among the literary sources which throw light on the degraded state of the Dalits is the *Manusmriti* (the Ordinances of Manu), which was possibly composed during the period A.D.1-700.[91] It is the author(s) of *Manusmriti*, who now onward even removed the human identity of the Dalits, who till then were considered outside the pale of the *chaturvarnyam*, but their existence at least was recognised. The *Manusmriti* accepts only the twice-born three castes: Brahman, Ksatriya and Vaisya, but the fourth, Sudra has only one birth. It says, "There is no fifth (caste)".[92] To explain the existence of those who were not of the four castes, *Manusmriti* put forward the concept of "mixed castes" which included those who were born out of intercaste marriages. The main divisions of such unions were named *anuloma,* where the male partner belonged to the upper caste and the female to the lower caste; and *pratiloma,* where the male partner belonged to the lower caste and the female to the upper caste. The offspring of *pratiloma* were considered most degraded.[93]

According to the *Manusmriti*, the most hated groups were *Chandala* and *Sapaka,* who were the offspring of a Sudra male from a Brahman woman, and *Chandala* male and a *Pukkasa* female respectively.[94] The *Manusmriti* 10.51.52 narrates the degraded non-human state of these groups in the following words:

> The dwelling of Chandalas and Cavpacas (sapaka) (should be) outside the village; they should be deprived of dishes (*apapatra*); their property (consists of) dogs and asses. Their clothes (should be) the garments of the dead, and their ornaments (should be) of iron, and their food (should be) in broken dishes; and they must constantly wander about.[95]

By the time the *Manusmriti's* composition was complete (around A.D. 700), the negative development of the Dalit state had reached its climax.

Against the supremacy of Brahmans even the revolt of Mahavira (540-468 B.C.) and Gautama Buddha (563-483 B.C.), the founders of Jainism and Buddhism, more or less failed.[96] About Gautama Buddha a French scholar, Luis Dumont says, "That Buddha himself, if he transcended caste, did not attack or reform it."[97] According to G.S. Ghurye "Thus Buddha is represented as being inclined to accept the divisions, basing them only in the individual's actions and not on his birth."[98] There is no doubt that Jainism and Buddhism were the first attacks or revolt in general against the caste system. But Dumont's observation also seems true, that "A sect cannot survive on Indian soil if it denies caste."[99] It was because of this phenomenon, according to Dumont, that Buddhism could not survive as a force beyond the fourteenth century. The Jain strategy to deal with the Hindu influence, according to Marcus Banks, "was to 'Hindu-ize'. Jinasena (a Digambara scholar ascetic) not only rewrote Hindu mythological history, he also included all the major Hindu *samskaras* (life-cycle rituals) within the Jain ritual system by giving them a Jain gloss." In fact "Jinasena created the notion of a Jain 'caste system', which he legitimated as an institution of Rishabhas."[100] In other words, even Jainism ultimately could not divest itself from the influence of the Hindu caste system. In Gujarat, even today two groups of Jains known as *Visa* and *Dasa* will not inter marry.[101] With such caste distinctions Jainism could contribute little to ameliorate the problem of the Dalits.

Buddhism faced a different kind of problem, because by the time of the *Manusmriti*, the followers of Gautama Buddha were also considered untouchables.[102] By and by Buddhism also got influenced by the caste system.[103] In post-Independence India, the hundreds of thousands of Mahar Dalits of Maharashtra who became Buddhists, in 1956 and later and their progeny are known as *Bauddh,* which in Marathi has become a synonym for Mahar (untouchable).[104] Thus the protest of Jainism and Buddhism, against Brahmanism or the caste system was in course of time diluted.

Later Developments

The period with which the discussion here is concerned, from A.D. 700 till date, can be divided broadly into three periods:

Muslim period, A.D. 700 to 1700
British period, A.D. 1700 to 1947
Post-Independence period, 1947 till date

Muslim Period

As seen above, by the time the *Manusmriti* (A.D. 700) reached its final literary form with its strict social and religious discipline to govern the graded Indian society, the religion of Prophet Mohammad also came into existence in the Arab world. The Arabs' first conquest of Sind was in A.D. 712, but only in A.D. 1206 the Slave Dynasty established its rule in Delhi. The Muslim invaders continued to come and go with their leaders like Sultan Mahmud of Ghazni and Muhammad Ghori. After the Slave Dynasty, India was ruled by different Muslim rulers and dynasties, such as Khiljis, Sayyids, Suris and Moghuls till the death of the last Mughal King Bahadur Shah in 1862.[105] During this long period of Muslim domination in India, one would have expected some changes in the lot of the Dalits as Islam upholds the principle of equality of all human beings.[106] But after going over the social and religious conditions of the Muslim period, one sees that more or less the state of the Dalits continues as before. Al-Biruni, writing on his visit to India around A.D. 1030, describes the treatment received by the Dalits as follows:

> The people called Hadi, Doma (Domba), Chandala, and Badhatau (*sic*) are not reckoned amongst any caste or guild. They are occupied with dirty work, like the cleaning of the villages and other services. They are considered like as one sole class, and distinguished only by their occupations. In fact, they are considered like illegitimate children; for according to general opinion they descended from a Sudra father and a Brahmani mother as the children of fornication; therefore they are degraded outcastes.[107]

More to the point, a number of well-known research works have confirmed that Muslim society itself was divided into a number of different grades/classes, though not exactly like the Hindu caste system. The highest grade, which was and is comparable to the Hindu "twice-born" upper castes were Ashrafs (meaning honourable), Shaikhs (chiefs) and Mughals and Pathans (corresponding to the Hindu Ksatriyas). The middle group was made up of those who have clean occupations. The last group included the converts from the untouchables, who do scavenging, sweeping and other menial tasks.[108] This division among the Muslims was confirmed by later historians and scholars who include J.S. Grewal.[109] J.S. Grewal has also observed that the differences

> on the basis of religion or race or occupation were reflected in the morphology of cities and towns. Urban centres were divided into separate quarters for the various social groups. On the outskirts of towns generally lived the scavengers, the leather dressers and the poor beggars. . .The respectable social groups among Muslims lived apart from the common populace. . . .[110]

Why did caste distinctions continue during the Muslim period in India and no change came even in the case of those Dalits who embraced Islam? "Acculturative influence of Hinduism" may be one reason. The other possible reasons "are those elements in Islam itself which support such distinctions". Imtiaz Ahmad, in the introduction to his edited work *Caste and Social Stratification among the Muslims,* has summarised these elements (based upon traditions) in these words:

> (a) an Arab was superior to a non-Arab,
>
> (b) among Arabs, all Quraishites were of equal social standing in a class by themselves, and all other Arabs were equal irrespective of their tribes,
>
> (c) among non-Arabs, a man was by birth the equal of Arabs, if both his father and grandfather were Muslims, but

only if he were sufficiently wealthy to provide an adequate *mahr* (endowment),

(d) a learned non-Arab was equal to an ignorant Arab, even if he was a descendant of Ali, "for the worth of learning is greater than the worth of family" and

(e) a Muslim Kazi or theologian ranked higher than a merchant, and a merchant higher than a tradesman.[111]

Different contributors to the above work have shown how even at present social distinctions among the Muslims continue in Bombay, Rajasthan, Haryana, Tamilnadu, Uttar Pradesh and West Bengal.

Besides Islam, during the Muslim period, there were other religions practised in India. The religions which came from outside India included Christianity, Judaism and Zoroastrianism. Christianity had already arrived before the Muslim presence got established here, and Judaism and Zoroastrianism came around the same time when Islam entered India. The indigenous religions which came into existence during the Muslim period were Lingayatism and Sikhism. Baha'i religion, which originated in Iran with its founder Baha'u'llah (1819-92), is to be found in the Malwa region of Central India.

Where Judaism is concerned, there have been two ancient settlements of Jews, one in Cochin (in South India in the state of Kerala) and the other in and around Bombay in the state of Maharashtra of Western India. Historically their presence in India is confirmed from A.D. 1020 onwards. This date is known from the date inscribed on a set of copper plates which were given to a Jewish leader named Joseph Rabban by a Hindu king. These copper plates had inscribed on them 72 privileges which he granted to the Jewish community. These included: "the right to ride an elephant, to be carried in a litter, to be preceded by drums and trumpets, to have a crier call out before their approach so that the lowly might withdraw from the streets".[112] Similar privileges were granted to a group of Syrian Christians by the same Hindu king, which thus gave both the communities the status of caste Hindus. Jewish scholar, Shalva Weil, says about this phenomenon:

In terms of the larger order of ranking, both these groups individually have had to internalise caste perceptions in order to provide legitimation for their ascribed status. As intermediaries in a ranked order of things between the local king and inferior castes, they have both, individually, shared what Fuller (1976) has termed a common "orthopraxy" with Hindus, while at the same retaining theoretical adherence to the egalitarianism of the Judeo-Christian tradition.[113]

Jews, both of Cochin and Bombay are divided into two main castes or *jatis* (groups) known as *Gora* (white) Jews and *Kala* (black) Jews According to Mandelbaum, these two groups of Jews, "did not interdine or intermarry, though they did worship in the same synagogues. Those of the higher *jati* claimed poorer Jewish ancestry. The lower, they alleged, was of mixed origins."[114] These facts were also confirmed during a visit to the Cochin Jewish community by the present author.[115] Shalva Weil also has confirmed that till 1950 there was a sizeable Jewish community in Cochin, but as most of these have migrated to Israel, their number now is very small.[116]

The other religious community which needs mention here are the Parsees, who are followers of Zoroastrianism. Their ancestors emigrated from Persia during seventh century A.D.[117] Eckehard Kulke has pointed out in his work *The Parsees in India* that Parsees before they came to India, were divided into four classes on the pattern of the Hindu caste system which were as follows:

Clergy (*Athravans* = Guardians of the fire)
—corresponding to the Brahmans among the Hindus.
Warriors (*Rathaeshtars* = He who is standing on a war-chariot)
—corresponding to the Ksatriyas.
Peasants (*Vactrya* = He who cultivates the land)
—corresponding to the Vaisyas.
Artisans (*Huiti* = Someone who produces objects)
—corresponding to the Sudras.[118]

The forefathers of the Parsees, when they emigrated to India were allowed by the local king Sanjan Jadi Rana to settle in a place named Sanjan in Gujarat, under certain strict conditions, which they accepted.[119] Since the Parsees did not believe in conversion,[120] there was very little chance for them to influence the social order in India based on the caste system. So Parsees or Zoroastrianism may be considered to be more or less unconcerned with the problem of the Dalits.

Lingayatism, or Veerasaivism as it is better known, is a religious sect whose heartland is northern Mysore in the state of Karnataka. Lingayatism is an egalitarian religion and the Lingayats treated everyone, including women as equal. Lingayats worship Shiva and according to their rule all members must always wear the Shiva emblem, the *lingam.* But according to Mandelbaum, Lingayats' *jatis* or groups are similar to those of Hindus. He says: "Despite the explicit rejection of caste-ordering in Lingayat scripture, Lingayats group themselves into ranked jatis. The highest are the Jangamas, hereditary priests and teachers."[121]

In any case, as Lingayatism was limited to a small part of one state, Karnataka in the south, and also since its followers were not free from the *Jati* distinctions, their role in the area of the Dalit problem is also limited.

The other religion which came into existence during the Muslim period was the Sikh religion, which also upholds the concept of egalitarianism.[122] The founder of the Sikh religion Nanak "did away altogether with caste distinctions and ceremonials".[123] But there are a number of testimonies available which show that by the time of the first half of the nineteenth century, the caste hierarchy among the Sikhs was well established.[124] While summing up the discussion on caste hierarchy among Sikhs, Ethne K. Marenco says:

> To sum up, therefore from the evidence of the Sikh Empire period, the many sources show that the Sikhs maintained caste practices, despite the fact that their religious dogma was against caste... The original conversion to Sikhism was striving for upward mobility, particularly when the lower Hindu caste converted. This type of corporate caste mobility, where whole groups convert to a religion that promises them an escape from their low caste position, has occurred more than once in India,

> and it was the phenomenon which was involved in the original conversion of Jat Hindus or Chuhra and Chamar Hindus or Chuhra Muslims (Mazhabis) to Sikhism.[125]

Marenco finally has observed that to some extent there is upward mobility among the Sikh Dalits, but it was not because they embraced Sikhism: "For the most part, their advance in Sikh society was due to the special favour they held with the British, on whose side they had fought during the Sepoy Mutiny."[126]

An egalitarian religion which came from outside is Baha'i. Its members are limited to Malwa villages in Central India and also it has got indigenised fully under the influence of Hindus. Therefore Baha'i egalitarian religion made very little positive contribution. A quotation from the work of W. Garlington will be helpful to clarify this point further:

> Therefore, by presenting Baha'u'llah as an *avatar* who has come to revitalise Hinduism rather than denounce it, Baha'i teachers do not make declarants forsake their Hindu heritage, and in effect they can psychologically remain Hindus: they are Hindus who believe in the Yugavatar, Baha'u'llah.[127]

Garlington adds:

> On the normative level the Baha'i Faith is an egalitarian religion, all believers are considered equal in the eyes of God, and therefore they all assume a similar status – that of God's servant. This ideal is in direct contrast to the traditional Hindu view as practised in Malva villages, whereby an individual is ranked according to his status group (caste) . . .[128]

British Period

The next important period of Indian history is the British. Technically this period began with the inauguration of the East India Company (London) in A.D. 1599.[129] But for the first 150 years the East India Company showed interest only in business and trade. It was only from A.D. 1744 onward that Lord Robert

Clive turned it into a military power.[130] In 1857 for the first time a major revolt took place in the Indian (British) army dominated mainly by upper castes which some of the historians see as the main reason for this revolt as it was a threat to the caste system and its practices. After crushing the revolt, the British with a proclamation of Queen Victoria in 1858 transferred political authority from the Company to the English Crown.[131]

During the British period a number of events took place, which finally led the country to freedom in 1947. As far as the religious and social practices were concerned, the British maintained the status quo and followed a policy of non-interference, "actively upholding and supporting the caste order".[132] "Even the protection of Caste was decreed by an Act of Parliament. In an order, it was declared, "due regard may be had to the civil and religious usages of the natives. . . ."[133]

The work of Christian missionaries in many ways has influenced the situation in India, particularly in challenging the various religious traditions to evaluate and rethink their approach to the poor and various Dalit groups.[134] But they also upheld the *varna* system. They even accepted it in the Christian Church.[135] When this was the case with both the British rulers and the Christian missionaries in general, one could expect very little from them which could be of help to the Dalits. More on this in the next chapter.

There was, however, one positive note. During the British period a number of small movements came into being, which showed concern for the Dalits. Before the British, during the Muslim period, the Bhakti Movement helped the cause of the Dalits, particularly in the spiritual sphere. This happened mostly through the Bhakti saints, who either were non-Brahmans or themselves were Dalits.[136] The efforts of most of these movements during the British period were limited to reform rather than aimed at total change.[137] But there were some personalities, who were involved directly in the struggle either for change or reform, who deserve mention here, because they certainly left their impact on the present Dalit movements. They include Jotiba Phule, Ambedkar and Gandhi. Among these, the first two were for the total uplift of the Dalits, Gandhi's work was limited to certain reforms, more within the Hindu society.

Ambedkar dedicated his work *Who were the Sudras* to Phule with these words:

Inscribed to the memory of Mahatma Jotiba Phule (1827-1890)

The Greatest Sudra of Modern India who made the lower classes among Hindus conscious of their slavery to the higher classes, and who preached the gospel that for India social democracy was more vital than independence from foreign rule.[138]

These words of Ambedkar are true to the spirit of Phule's pioneering work. The important phrase to be noted is "who made the lower classes of Hindus conscious of their slavery".

Phule belonged to the Mali caste, and had little education. In 1873 he started an association named Satyashodhak Samaj with the definite purpose of "asserting the worth of man irrespective of caste." He encouraged through his writings a revolt against "the tyranny of the caste system." His revolt was "against caste in so far as caste denied ordinary human rights to all." In 1851 he started a primary school for the so-called untouchables in Poona.[139] He criticised the *Manusmriti* because he realised that it was the greatest stumbling block in the way of social change.[140] Phule "made efforts to unite all the non-Brahmin"[141] Dalits.

The efforts Ambedkar and Gandhi made with regard to the Dalits during the British period are also important. In a real sense they were opposing one another in this struggle. This is known through the different approaches they adopted in dealing with the British on the question of the Dalits. This well-known struggle of theirs was another glaring example of the Dalits' problems and it had an impact on the history of the Dalits for years to come.

As mentioned earlier, a number of reform movements including those by Christian missionaries[142] were at work for the betterment of the Dalits, which ultimately also influenced the British Government to do something in this regard. During this period new titles and phrases were coined to denote the Dalits. For example, for the first time the existence of the "Depressed classes" was recognised in the text of the Act of 1919.[143] In 1931, the

Census Superintendent of Assam made a suggestion to change this title the Depressed Classes to the "Exterior Castes". The argument for this suggestion was that it is a broader title, because its connotation does not limit itself to "outcaste" people (which means people who are outside the caste system). On the other hand, Exterior Castes would include those who had been cast out because of some breach of caste rules.[144] More pertinent to our discussion, and the struggle of the Dalits, is the term "Scheduled Castes", which was first coined by the Simon Commission (appointed by the British Government) and embodied in the Government of India Act, 1935, in Section 305.[145]

Prior to this coinage, the term 'Depressed Classes' was used in government circles and also by members of various reform movements. But till 1932 the latter expression was used more or less for all kinds of "depressed" people including the "untouchables". Also till then no effort was made to define this term on a religious basis. It was in 1932 that for the first time the expression "Depressed Classes" was used exclusively for people with an Untouchable background. The British Government, which was at that time also trying to help all other minority communities such as Muslims, Christians, Anglo-Indians, and so on, excluded them from the definition of Depressed Classes, while bestowing on them special benefits, such as giving them separate communal electorates. In 1931 a special committee was also set up to draw a "Schedule" of the castes and classes covered under the Depressed Classes. Also at that time in 1931, the Round Table Conference was called in London.

At the Round Table Conference, Gandhi and Ambedkar were the key members. Ambedkar demanded a separate electorate for the Depressed Classes, whom he always referred to as the "Untouchables". At this conference, he also proposed that the Untouchables be called "Protestant Hindus" or "Non-conformist Hindus".[146] But Gandhi objected to Ambedkar's demand for a separate electorate. By that time, of course, Gandhi had also introduced his favourite term "Harijan" to be used in place of Untouchable, which was not accepted or liked by the untouchables themselves.[147] As Gandhi and Ambedkar did not agree with each other at the Round Table Conference, no final decision was taken.

Finally, the whole matter of a separate communal electorate was left to the chairman of the conference, Prime Minister Ramsay Macdonald, who in 1932 issued the Communal Award. In this he also replaced the expression "Depressed Classes" with "Scheduled Castes". (From then on the Untouchables of India were known as "Scheduled Castes"). Later the same expression was included in the Government of India (Scheduled Castes) Order, 1936.[148] Gandhi opposed the Communal Award in the case of the Scheduled Castes because of the fear of their getting separated from Hindu society in general.[149] Therefore he went on a fast unto death for which nobody was willing to take the responsibility. Even Ambedkar had to bow and agree to alter the Communal Award in a manner satisfactory to Gandhi.[150] According to this agreement in place of a "separate electorate", "joint" electorate for the Scheduled Castes with the caste Hindu majority was accepted. This, according to Upendra Baxi, was a defeat for the political liberal Ambedkar by his shrewd opponent Gandhi."Gandhi gambled on Ambedkar's self-restraint and won", says Baxi and "the costs of the victory would have to be recorded by Untouchable historians of future India."[151] In this way one more chance of effective liberation and freedom was lost by the Dalits. But Ambedkar at least got a larger number of seats for the Dalits, which of course was an achievement.[152]

Post-Independence Period

The problem of the Dalits and the struggle for liberation is continuing in the post-Independence period with equal fervour, because even India's political freedom in 1947 was not able to help them in getting out of their condition. Prior to Independence, the British rulers used the policy of "non-interference" in local, cultural and religious practices, in order to rule the people of India, and for that they even created a new vocabulary. The new rulers of independent India have continued to use the same vocabulary and expressions which in no way have helped the masses, particularly the Dalits.

This was perhaps the reason why most of the Dalit movements

and their leaders were not supportive of the freedom movement led by the upper castes under the Indian National Congress.[153] While piloting the Constitution of independent India on November 4, 1948 Ambedkar did say it was "workable" and "flexible" but even this character of the Constitution has been used only to maintain the status quo of the set rules of life in Indian society because it has only gone in favour of the powerful, not the mass of powerless people. The Constitution itself, as Ambedkar said, is not "bad", it is the use of its flexibility which has proved bad. It is because of this truth, that the condition of the Dalits, even after Independence, has not improved. In order to clarify this a few examples are considered and discussed from the post-Independence (1947) efforts. This discussion will be confined to three major examples, which hopefully will help to understand the issue:

I. The Constitution (Scheduled Castes) Order, 1950.
II. Report of the first Commissioner for Scheduled Castes and Scheduled tribes for the period ending 31st December, 1951.
III. Report of the Backward Classes Commission, 1980 (popularly known as Mandal Commission).

The Constitution (Scheduled Castes) Order, 1950

The Indian Constitution as per Article 341 (1) empowers the President of India, "... by public notification, (to) specify the castes, races or tribes or parts or of groups within castes, races or tribes which shall, for the purpose of this Constitution be deemed to be Scheduled Castes ..."[154] Again the Constitution, without defining in Article 366(24) only refers back to the power given to the President of India in Article 341.[155] But once the President has given such an order, this list prepared on the basis of Article 342(2) or Scheduled Castes can be changed only through an Act of Parliament.

While exercising the powers conferred in Article 341(1) on him, the President of India promulgated an Order in 1950, known as The Constitution (Scheduled Castes) Order, 1950. In the list of the Scheduled Castes this order almost re-enacted the list of the Government of India (Scheduled Castes) Order, 1936.[156]

Concerning the Scheduled Caste people the Constitution has followed the basis the British Government laid down in 1936. This applies not only to the list, but also the criterion, which the British Government used to define "Scheduled Caste", because the same is followed for the Order of 1950. On that basis the third paragraph of this Order reads: "Notwithstanding anything contained in paragraph 2, no person who professes a religion different from Hindu, shall be deemed to be a member of a Scheduled Caste." This paragraph was changed in 1956 by Parliament to "Hindu or Sikh" and again in May 1990 to "Hindu or Sikh or Buddhist".

So the positions of the President and Parliament are the same as that of the British Government in 1932-36, because it has used "religion" as the criterion to define the Scheduled Castes, but a political party like the Bharatiya Janata Party (BJP) has a still more orthodox and biased criterion in regard to the Scheduled Castes, or the Dalits. On June 12, 1990 at Thiruvananthapuram in South India, a senior leader of the BJP, L.K. Advani stated his party's criterion on this question, which was reported by the *Indian Express*:

> The BJP leader, however, said that his party was stoutly opposed to any move by the V.P. Singh government to extend reservation to converts to Islam and Christianity from Scheduled Castes and Scheduled Tribes. It had supported the extension of reservation to SC/ST converts to Buddhism because under the Constitution Buddhists and Sikhs and Jains were classified as Hindus. Reservation to converts to other religions would violate the recommendation of the Constituent Assembly, he added.[157]

This is the basic contradiction India has, which the Constitution of the country and those responsible for its implementation are faced with, because the view expressed above, and decisions based on such views, not only violate the fundamental rights (Article 15.1), they also raise the question of human rights based on the principle of equality (see for detailed discussion Chapter Four).

Regarding the criterion, the point made by Ram Vilas Paswan needs to be noted. Paswan, who was then Union Minister of Welfare and Labour, made the remark while stating the objects and reasons for proposing to include neo-Buddhist converts from Scheduled Caste background in the list of Scheduled Castes. He said:

> "New-Buddhists" are a religious group which has come into existence in 1956 as a result of a wave of conversions of the Scheduled Castes under the leadership of Dr. Babasaheb Ambedkar. Upon conversion to Buddhism, they became ineligible for statutory concessions . . . Various demands have been made . . . for extending all the concessions and facilities available to the Scheduled Castes to them also *on the ground that change of religion has not altered their social and economic conditions*. . . . As they objectively deserve to be treated as Scheduled Castes for the purpose of various reservations, it is proposed to amend the Presidential Orders to include them therein.[158]

In May 1990 the amendment was passed by Parliament and now neo-Buddhists also get the same concessions which Scheduled Castes belonging to the Hindu and Sikh religion were getting. But the point here is that the basis of this amendment has changed from what the 1950 Order says about "religion".

The Presidential Order looks good on the surface from all aspects, but if one looks deep into the spirit of this Order, one realises how it has become the basis for the continuity of the Dalits' problem, supported by the powerful religious lobby. As far as the Constitution is concerned, one may agree with Ambedkar that there is nothing bad in it, because it rightly maintained the spirit of secularism while guaranteeing full freedom of religion to every citizen (Articles 25, 26, 28, 30), and it also has forbidden any kind of discrimination by the State on the basis of religion (Articles 15, 16, 29, 325). But then, the above Presidential Order had not only violated the sacred spirit of these Articles of the Constitution, but also has literally gone against every word of these articles. Interestingly, to commit these constitutional violations, the Supreme Head of the country has been used.

The other fact which needs to be noted is that by adding in the Presidential Order the term "Hindu" in 1950, once again officially, India as a nation, constitutionally has upheld the system of caste (*varna*). In this way what Gandhi won through his "fast unto death" in 1932 has been won in post-Independence India by those interested in carrying on such a system through the Presidential Order.

Somehow, for more than four decades now, the Dalits have also fallen into this trap. On the other hand, those who have not fallen into the trap have been deprived even of their basic human rights or equality, including constitutional fundamental rights. The best examples of this are the Christian and Muslim Dalits. (Detailed discussion of this point is found in Chapter Five). To some extent, the Sikh Dalits and the Buddhist Dalits have won their rights and in a way have paved the way for others. But it seems, for the fuller restoration of the human rights of the Dalits, they have to still wait and work.

Report of the first Commissioner for Scheduled Castes and Scheduled Tribes for the period ending 31st December, 1951

The Constitution of India also empowers the Government in Article 338(1) to appoint a Special Officer for the Scheduled Castes and Scheduled Tribes. This Article in the second clause states the duty of the Special Officer in these words:

> It shall be the duty of the Special Officer to investigate all matters relating to the safeguards provided for the Scheduled Castes and Scheduled Tribes under the Constitution and report to the President on the working of those safeguards at such intervals as the President may direct, and the President shall cause all such reports to be laid before each House of Parliament.[159]

Under this Article the President of India appointed L.M.

Shrikant as the first Commissioner (Special Officer) on November,18, 1950, with the responsibility stated in the second clause of Article 338. This work is concerned with the Dalits (Scheduled Castes) and with that part of the report of L.M. Shrikant covering the period up to December 31, 1951, which helps in knowing the state of the Dalits in the early period of post-Independence. Shrikant opens his report with these words, which are worth noting:

> Caste in Hindu society is still the most powerful factor in determining a man's dignity, calling or profession. Such a rigid caste system is not found anywhere else outside India. All such professions involve handling of the so-called dirty jobs like tanning and skinning of hides, manufacture of leather goods, sweeping of streets, scavenging, etc. allotted to some castes, also known as Harijans, who are about 5 crores according to the latest figures available.[160]

The most important statement of the report is found on the opening page. It reads as follows:

> By the force of habit the Harijan (Dalit) has lost his self-respect to such an extent that he regards his work to which his caste is condemned not as a curse from which he should extricate himself but as a privilege or preserve, which he must protect. He has not much courage to seek another job in field or factory. He has thus become lazy in mind and body and callous to his own condition; and he will not educate his children.[161]

These words reveal the inner nature of the *dalitness* (state) of the Dalits which they have reached by the ongoing oppression of the caste and the social system which Indian society continues to maintain. Part of the statement reads that a Dalit "has lost his self-respect to such an extent that he regards his work to which his caste is condemned not as a curse from which he should extricate himself but as a privilege. . . " These words also reveal the power of the caste system which can transform the person into such a self-captivity or a slavery from which it seems almost impossible to be liberated. The second important truth about the Dalits that Shrikant has stated is that the Dalit has "become lazy in mind and body, callous to his own condition". Of course being "lazy in mind" and to feel "callous" for his/her own condition are part of the inner nature or *dalitness* of the Dalits which really is responsible for many problems of the Dalits, which cannot simply be dealt with by mere passing of legislation or providing economic facilities. Shrikant has provided one possible suggestion to deal with the problem, namely "education" which he says, a Dalit is not willing to give to his children. This non-willingness is again part of the inner nature of *dalitness,* which needs to be dealt with first, when one talks of making a provision for the education of Dalit children.

Shrikant, as the first Commissioner, undertook an extensive tour to get first hand information about the Dalits, on whom he spent much space in his report, describing what he had observed and had seen personally. For example, about the implementation of the Social Disabilities Removal Acts adopted by various states, he says that very few crimes committed against the Dalits have come to light. According to him,

> The main reason for this is that Harijans (Dalits) have no courage to come forward either to draw water from the common wells or to go to shops, public restaurants, hotels etc., as they are generally economically dependent on non-Harijans in one way or the other. At places where offences committed under these Acts have not been made cognizable, it is very difficult for the Scheduled Caste people to take any action against culprits because the police are incapable of taking any action if a report is made to them.[162]

Shrikant's view again gets support from the Report of the Commissioner for Scheduled Castes and Scheduled Tribes of April 1985-March 1986. This report, 35 years after the first report of 1951, proves that these atrocities against the Dalits continue as in 1950-51 or before.[163] Even the later Commissioners observed that while 15 per cent of the posts were reserved for the Scheduled Castes, only 2.2 per cent were filled.[164]

These Commissioners' reports show that historically the development of the Dalits' problem is continuing on the same pattern as in the past. It is because no effort has been made to change the religious-*cum*-social-*cum*-cultural features of Indian society that the Dalits' problem is perpetuated.

Report of the Backward Classes Commission, 1980 (popularly known as Mandal Commission)

Marc Galanter helps in understanding the underlying values of the Mandal Commission Report when he opens his work on *Competing Equalities: Law and the Backward Classes in India*, with these words:

> India's system of preferential treatment for historically disadvantaged sections of the population is unprecedented in scope and extent. India embraced equality as a cardinal value against a background of elaborated, valued, and clearly perceived inequalities. Her constitutional policies to offset these proceeded from an awareness of the entrenched and cumulative nature of group inequalities. The result has been an array of programmes that I call, collectively, a policy of compensatory discrimination.[165]

Galanter's statement is possibly the best summary of the Mandal Commission's efforts. Mandal and other Commissions' reports are part of an array of programmes launched by the Indian Government to uplift those people or citizens of India, who in the history of India, have been kept forcibly and systematically at a disadvantage. To deal with this historical evil, which is an ongoing reality in the Indian society, independent India accepted "equality as a cardinal value" for all her citizens. The truth has been stated right in the Preamble of our Constitution. Also, as mentioned earlier Articles 15.1-3 and 16.1-3 offer "equality" as a fundamental right to all citizens of India.

But in the same Articles, clauses 15.4 and 16.4 make a special provision for the care of those citizens who are socially and educationally backward, along with the Scheduled Castes and

Scheduled Tribes. Article 38 under the Directive Principles of State Policy states it clearly that it is the duty of the State to promote the welfare of the people by securing a just and equitable social order. In the same Article in clause 2 it is also said: "That the State shall, in particular, strive to minimise the inequalities in income, and endeavour to eliminate inequalities in status, facilities and opportunities. . . ." The constitutional declaration under Article 38.1 also has an implied meaning that there was an unjust order in India before the advent of the Indian Constitution. Also the Constitution, through its Article 46 has placed an obligation on the State for the special care of the weaker sections of people in areas of economic and educational interests and for their protection from social injustice and all forms of exploitation. It has also made provision for how to deal with the whole situation. For example, Article 341 takes care of Scheduled Castes and Scheduled Tribes (already referred to) and Article 340 deals with the question of "socially and educationally backward classes". Article 340 gives power to the President of India to appoint a Commission to investigate the condition of the people of backward classes and also recommend steps which can help improve their condition.

Under Article 340, the first Backward Classes Commission was appointed by the President on January 29, 1953 with Kakasaheb Kalelkar as its chairman. This Commission submitted its report on March 30, 1955.[166] The task of the Commission included determining the criteria for identifying sections of people who could be included in the list of Backward Classes, and also to suggest steps to improve their condition. About the criteria for identifying the classes, this Commission suggested "caste" as a criterion, on which all the members of the Commission did not agree.[167] At the same time, the Central Government also could not fully agree with its recommendation, so it came to the conclusion that no all-India list of backward classes was possible. Ultimately the Central Government told the State Governments, that they could fix their own criteria for defining backwardness and prepare a list of Backward Classes. As a result a number of states, Andhra Pradesh, Bihar, Gujarat, Uttar Pradesh and Tamil Nadu, set up their state level commissions. Eight other states and Union territories also notified their lists of Backward Classes. They are:

Assam, Delhi, Haryana, Himachal Pradesh, Meghalaya, Orissa, Pondicherry and Rajasthan. All these states fixed their reservation quotas for the Backward Classes between 66 per cent (which is the highest, in Karnataka) and 5 per cent (which is the lowest, in Punjab) in government services, and educational institutions.[168]

The second Backward Classes Commission (known as Mandal Commission, 1980), under the chairmanship of the late B.P. Mandal, was officially appointed on January 1, 1979, and the report of the Commision was submitted on December 31, 1980. Besides presenting the report to the President, the Commission's main tasks included, (1) to determine the criteria for defining the socially and educationally backward classes, (2) to recommend steps to be taken for the advancement of the socially and educationally backward classes of citizens so identified, and (3) to examine the desirability or otherwise of making provision for the reservation of appointments or posts in favour of such backward classes which are not adequately represented in public services and posts in connection with the affairs of the Union or of any state.[169]

The Mandal Commission before making its recommendations, made a thorough analysis of the causes of the backwardness of those sections of the people whom it ultimately recommended to be included in the list. According to the Commission, the caste system is the root cause of all kinds of backwardness. Its effects have gone right into the being of people. It says: "The real triumph of the caste system lies not in upholding the supremacy of the Brahmin, but in conditioning the consciousness of the Lower Castes in accepting their inferior status in the ritual hierarchy as part of the natural order of things."[170]

In the Commission's view the caste system is not merely a social phenomenon, it is a well worked out scheme based on scripture, mythology, rituals. According to it:

> The above scheme of social organisation, transfixed for over 3,000 years, had far-reaching effects on the growth and development of various castes and communities. For instance, as exclusive custodians of higher knowledge, the Brahmins grew into a highly cultivated community with a special flair for

> intellectual pursuits. On the other hand, the Sudras, being continuously subjected to all sorts of social, educational, cultural and economic deprivation, acquired all the unattractive traits of unlettered rustics.[171]

The Commission's discussion on the "Social Dynamics of Caste" makes it clear "that despite the resolve of our Constitution-makers to establish a casteless society, the importance of caste has increased in some of the most important spheres of our national life".[172] The Commission has also recognised the weakening aspects of the caste system, particularly where the traditional features of the caste system are concerned. But to this fact the Commission adds a note of caution in these words:

> But what caste has lost on the ritual front, it has more than gained on the political front. This has led to some adjustments in the power equation between the high and low castes and thereby accentuated social tensions. Whether these tensions rent the social fabric or the country is able to resolve them by internal adjustments will depend on how understandingly the ruling high castes handle the legitimate aspirations and demands of the historically suppressed and backward classes.[173]

According to the Mandal Commission Report the institution of caste contains in it a large "element of inequality and discrimination".[174] The principle of equality is the factor which the Commission has considered important for the understanding of the condition of the people belonging to backward classes. About this principle the Report says: "On the face of it the principle of equality appears very just and fair, but it has a serious catch. It is a well known dictum of social justice that there is equality only amongst equals. To treat unequals as equals is to perpetuate inequality."[175]

Here the Commission has raised a vital question which actually leads towards a contradiction of interests between fundamental rights, which are individualistic in nature, and the interests of society, which are given under thr Directive Principles of State Policy. Also the Commission's overall concerns relating to Article 15.4, it seems, are also in direct conflict with the fundamental rights. But this conflict is there, or at least has been felt from the beginning, since the Constitution came into existence. The Commission quotes from a debate which went on at the time of the First Amendment Bill in 1951, when Jawaharlal Nehru highlighted this conflict in these words:

> . . . If in the protection of individual liberty, you protect also individual or group inequality, then you come into conflict with the Directive Principle which wants, according to your Constitution, a gradual advance or let us put it another way, not so gradual but more rapid advance, whenever possible, to a state where there is less inequality and more and more equality. If any kind of an appeal to the continuation of the existing inequality is made, then you get into difficulties. Then you become static, the idea of an egalitarian society which I hope most of us aim at.[176]

Nehru's words help us to see the positive side of The Mandal Commission's Report. Regarding the tests of a just and equitable order, the Commission also is clear that both equality of opportunity and of treatment are not real tests. About the first it says, "Equality of opportunity promised under Article 16(1) of the Constitution is actually a liberation and not an egalitarian principle as it allows the same freedom to everybody in the race of life."[177] About the second, the Commission quotes from H.B. Gans (*More Equality*, New York, 1973), who says, ". . . equality of treatment suffers from the same drawback as equality of opportunity for to treat the disadvantaged uniformly with the advantaged, will only perpetuate their disadvantage."[178] The Commission talks about the third test also, about which it says:

> If a tree is to be judged by its fruits, equality of results is obviously the most reliable test of our aspiration and efforts to establish a just and equitable order. A formidable task under any circumstances, it becomes particularly so in a society which has remained segmented in a finely graded caste hierarchy for centuries.[179]

About questions of "merit" and "privilege", the Commission makes a concluding remark in these words:

> In fact, what we call merit in an elitist society is an amalgam of native endowments and environmental privileges. . . The conscience of a civilized society and the dictates of social justice demand that 'merit' and 'equality' are not turned into a fetish and the element of privilege is duly recognised and discounted for when "unequals" are made to run the same race.[180]

On August 7, 1990 when the former Prime Minister V.P. Singh announced the implementation of the Mandal Commission Report (of course only partly), it shook Indian society to its very foundations. The various assessments and views both "for" and "against" were pronounced and are being pronounced even after-wards. Two such pronouncements are referred to here: the *Indian Express* (August 18, 1991) published two short articles under the title "Is Mandal still a burning issue" by S.S. Gill "for", and Hiranmay Karlekar "against". Both the articles can be summed up by two expressions used by the two writers, "Mandalisation is basically a question of sharing power. . ." and "It was clearly a cynical political move. . ." respectively.[181] To some extent, both these writers are correct: "sharing power" and "a cynical political move" are in a way judgements upon those who try to implement the Mandal Commission with their own agenda before them, but where the Dalits are concerned, the struggle about the Mandal Commission Report or its recomendations are really a part of the age-old struggle of oppressed human beings who, for more than 3,000 years, have been losing. This fact has been stated by a number of thinkers. For example, Brindavan Moses on September 15, 1990 in the *Economic and Political Weekly* wrote:

> The extremely disturbing fact to be reckoned with in this context is that the upper and middle classes are not merely up in arms against the proposed reservations for the backward classes/castes in government jobs, but are also asserting their right to overlordship in perpetuity over those whom they treat with contempt as the incompetent and unqualified.[182]

Gail Omvedt put the same issue differently, but in more aggressive language.

> Writing on the Mandal Commission and the "caste war" going on around it. . . The twice born outnumber the Dalits and Sudras in the forums which produce the war of words, but the Dalits and Sudras outnumber the twice-born in the street. . .[183]

There are many other conflicting views about the Mandal Commission which show that the struggle in which opposing forces or groups were or are involved, is not about a few thousand jobs, it was actually about the very being of two different groups of people—on one side a "being" who thousands of years ago enslaved the others, and on the other side a "being" who now has awakened or is awakening out of his/her enslavement and is struggling to get out of it. Besides, the Mandal Commission Report brings out the role of religion while linking it with the past, and how it continues in the present to contribute to the development of the Dalit problem.

Are Dalits Indigenous People?

To begin this section, a question can be raised: who are the indigenous people? The report of the first Commissioner for Scheduled Castes and Scheduled Tribes, L.M. Shrikant gave three main characteristics which, according to him are applicable to all the Scheduled Tribes of India:

(a) primitive way of living,

(b) habitation in remote and less easily accessible areas.

(c) nomadic habits and love of drink and dance.[184]

He also invited comments in order to establish some definite criteria for identifying the Scheduled Tribes. After receiving comments from the states, he fixed the following criteria without giving any explanation:

(a) tribal origin;

(b) primitive way of life and habitation in remote and less easily accessible areas; and

(c) general backwardness in all respects.[185]

It would have been better if Shrikant could have gone back to the history of the origins of these people for the above purpose; then he could have also understood why they are still living in remote areas and why they are backward in all respects. Answers to these questions could have helped also in establishing the relationship between indigenous people and the Dalits. This information, at the same time, could have helped in defining the term "indigenous", especially its use for a particular group of people in society. In the absence of such information, one may look into some agreed international views with regard to "indigenous" people, which will clear the question whether there exists any relationship between the Dalits of India and the indigenous people of India. Here for the purpose of this study, a Report of the Independent Commission on International Humanitarian Issues (ICIHI) on indigenous peoples of the world, which appeared as a printed document in 1987 is being referred to. ICIHI listed the following four major elements in the definition of indigenous people: pre-existence (that is, the population are descendants of those inhabiting an area prior to the arrival of another population); non-dominance, cultural differences; and self-identification as indigenous. ICIHI also adds: "The most undisputed criterion is that indigenous people are the descendants of the original inhabitants of the territory taken over through conquest or settlement by aliens."[186]

It is true, there is no universally accepted definition of indigenous people. But a definition which is being used by the United Nations, (developed by Special Rapporteur on the Problem of Discrimination against Indigenous Population for the United Nations Sub-Commission on Prevention of Discrimination and Protection of Minorities) could be of further help in understanding the criterion for identifying indigenous people in the Indian situation. The Special Rapporteur has included also "isolated and marginal population" as indigenous, even if they have not suffered conquest or colonisation directly.[187] The Special Rapporteur, in 1982, while recognising that the right of defining what and who is indigenous belongs to the indigenous peoples themselves, has proposed the following definition:

> Indigenous communities, peoples and nations are those which, having an historical continuity with pre-invasion and pre-colonial societies that developed on their territories, consider themselves distinct from other sectors of these societies now prevailing in those territories, or part of them. They form at present non-dominant sectors of society and are determined to preserve, develop and transmit to future generations their ancestral territories, and their ethnic identity, as the basis of their continued existence as peoples, in accordance with their own cultural patterns, social institutions and legal systems.[188]

In principle, the Dalits themselves have to decide if they are indigenous or not. But if one looks at the four major elements given above, and the definition of indigenous peoples, these three—pre-existence, non-dominance and cultural differences—are applicable to the Dalits, as also to the indigenous groups (particularly groups in Bihar and central India known as *adivasi*). Only the fourth element, namely, "self identification as indigenous" may be questioned, but the answer to this question is found in their forgotten history; an attempt has been made to reconstruct it in the previous sections of this chapter. At this point another question may be raised about the Dalits being indigenous and their present relationship with land and its natural resources, which are considered divine by indigenous people—"gifts entrusted to them for safe-keeping and for passing on intact to future generations".[189] It is true, this custodial attitude, as it were, is missing among the Dalits, but here one needs to remember (as pointed out in the earlier sections), that during the last more than 3,000 years too many generations have passed for the present generations to remember that possibly once the land and its natural resources belonged to their ancestors, where now they live landless and resourceless. With this long time gap and the kind of oppression they have undergone or are facing, their attitude not only towards land and natural resources, but also towards themselves (towards their very being) possibly has changed, which they have now accepted "as a part of the natural order of things" (words of the Mandal Commission) or which now they have accepted "as a privilege" (words of L.M. Shrikant).

Before taking this point of discussion further, on this question of the Dalits being indigenous people, it may be worth stating that a number of writers' comments hint directly or indirectly that the Dalits once were, in real fact, a part of the communities of people who today fall under the category of indigenous. These scholars include Stephen Fuchs,[190] Hugh Kennedy Trevaskis,[191] Romila Thapar,[192] Prabhati Mukherjee,[193] G.S. Ghurye,[194] N.K. Dutt[195] and Niharranjan Ray.[196]

Besides the indirect or direct comments of these writers which help to link the roots of the Dalits with a large number of indigenous groups known as *adivasis* (living in the central part of India), three works of other writers have dealt in detail with the question of "Dalits being an indigenous people". These are Ambedkar, Suresh Narain Srivastava and J. Van Troy. But before moving to their works, it should also be mentioned here that the two main sources— the *Rigveda* and the archaeological sources also extend support to this contention.

In the hymns of the *Rigveda*, there are a number of references which draw attention to the defeated indigenous groups, and how after their defeat they were either forced to scatter or they themselves willingly got scattered in different directions. Some of the references in this regard are found in hymns 2.20.7, 4.28.4, 6.25.2, 6.69.6, 7. 5.3 etc.[197] Where evidence from the works of archaeologists is concerned, this has been quoted already, namely the works of Ernest Mackay, and George F. Dales in earlier sections and which hint at the shift or movement of people from Northwest India (Mohenjodaro and Harappa) to other parts of India.

Coming back to the works of the three scholars, Ambedkar has discussed this question in his work *The Untouchables* (1948), with a question: Who were they and why they became Untouchables? The first point about Ambedkar's work that needs to be remembered is what he himself has said about it: "This book may, therefore, be taken as a pioneer in the exploration of a field so completely neglected by everybody."[198] So while considering his views here, one needs to take them as "pioneer" in nature, which also demands further work in the field of the history of the untouchables or the Dalits.

Ambedkar's work is based on his thesis that there is no racial difference between the Untouchables (Dalits) and other groups or castes. According to Ambedkar, the divisions in Indian society began with a primitive society which consisted of many local communities (or tribes). In the beginning, all these communities were nomadic. But with time and because of intra-tribal warfare, they got divided into three groups: a Settled Community, a Raider Community belonging to nomadic tribes, and a Broken Men's community consisting of defeated people of defeated tribes. The last group is important, because it is these Broken Men, according to Dr. Ambedkar, who at a later stage were turned into Untouchables or today's Dalits. These Broken Men were the people of defeated tribes, who with their defeat got scattered or broken up from their original tribes.[199]

Ambedkar's pioneering effort to deal with the roots of the Dalits (Untouchables) is important, because besides throwing light on how the Dalits have reached their present state, it also puts forward another important point at the beginning—today's so called "Criminal Tribes", "Aboriginal Tribes" and "the Untouchables" (Dalits) had a common beginning.[200] (See also Chapter Three for this point.)

Suresh Narain Srivastava's work *Harijans in Indian Society* (1980) adds clarity to this concern of the "Dalits being indigenous". Besides considering most of the possible literary sources, he also takes into account the archaeological findings concerning Mohenjodaro and Harappa and has come to clear conclusions, which are helpful in settling this issue. The following two quotations from Srivastava's work may be sufficient for our purpose:

> The pre-Dravidian settlers were the natives of India. . . . The Dravidians were the first to have attacked the Aboriginals of India. . . they did not make aboriginals their own slaves. . . . After the Dravidians, another major attack was made by the Aryans. . . . As the victorious people, the Aryan invaders looked down upon their opponents and called them the Dasa-Dasyus and the Nishadas.[201]

Srivastava in his work further elaborates:

> Therefore, defeated aboriginals were made 'slaves' in the social order. . . These slaves have been included in the fold of Hinduism by placing them on the lowest rung of the social ladder. . . Those who did not accept the offer of becoming slaves, were driven away into forests and they remained aboriginals with their social, economic and cultural distinctions. . . . In the course of time, these people were divided into two classes. Some became nomadic tribes and others roaming from place to place. These roaming peoples were called criminal tribes. . . . In this way, an ancient Indian society came to be divided into four parts—the Aryans, the non-Aryans, the aboriginals and the nomadic criminal tribes."[202]

In the second quotation, the last two lines make one point clear—while leaving out the first groups of Aryans, the other three groups of people, the non-Aryans (today's Dalits), the aboriginals (today's indigenous people) and the nomadic criminal tribes (today's communities of groups, who still roam around) have the same roots. In other words these later three groups are in a real sense the people of indigenous origin, because their forefathers were the same.

The third work is an article included in *Cultural Chotanagpur—Unity in Diversity* edited by S. Bosu-Mullick, 1991, "Pre-history and Early History of Chotanagpur" by J. Van Troy. Van Troy attempts to establish a historical relationship between the people of Chotanagpur (indigenous) known as *Kurukh* or *Oraons* with their past history. He has taken into account archaeological and linguistic evidence. There are two possibilities: first, the forefathers of Oraons were the descendants of the pre-Harappa people; second, the Oraons came from Northwest India. The latter view is based on linguistic evidence.[203] Van Troy's article has not given any final conclusion, but it certainly raises the possibility of establishing a link between the indigenous people of Chotanagpur and those who once lived in the ancient part of India known today as Northwest India. This attempt definitely points towards a close relationship between the Dalits and the indigenous people and ultimately their having common forefathers.

On the basis of the discussion and various views, it may be said that the Dalits share their historical roots with the indigenous people, particularly groups known as *adivasis*.

Concluding Remarks

Three main points become clear on the historical roots of the Dalits of India:

First, the Dalits are descendants of the earliest settlers of India.

Second, the history of the Dalits' present problem began around 1500 B.C. and for more than 3,500 years they have suffered and continue to suffer multiple oppressions, which have always been supported by religion, directly or indirectly.

Third (and which is most important), because of the long history of oppression the Dalits have even lost their self-identity as full human beings, which they have now accepted "as a part of the natural order of things" or "as a privilege" and this in a real sense is the inner captivity of their being from which they need liberation or release.

NOTES AND REFERENCES

1. (a) Wheeler, Sir Mortimer: *The Cambridge History of India, Supplementary Volume, The Indus Civilization,* Cambridge, 1953, p. 86.
   (b) Kapur Singh: 'Mohenjodaro' in *Pundreek* (Punjabi) Ambala, 1952, p. 145.
2. Basham, A.L.: "The Aryan Problem" in R.C. Majumdar and A.D. Pusalkar (eds.), *The History and Culture of the India People, The Vedic Age,* London, 1951, p. 204.
3. (a) Srivastava, Suresh Narain: *Harijans in Indian Society,* Lucknow, 1980, pp. 1 ff.
   (b) Kapur Singh: *op.cit.,* p. 201ff.
   (c) Ambedkar, B.R.: "The Untouchables, Who were they and why they became Untouchables" in *Dr. Babasaheb Ambedkar, Writings and Speeches,* edited by Vasant Moon, Vol. 7, Bombay, 1990, p. 275.
   (d) Smith, Vincent A: *The Oxford History of India,* Oxford, 1958, p. 32.
   (e) Basham A.L: *op.cit.,* p. 29.
   (f) Chattopadhyaya, K.P.: *The Indian Culture Contacts and Migrations,* Calcutta, 1970, p. 6.

(g) Chanda, Ramaprasad: *The Indo-Aryan Races, A study of the Origin of Indo-Aryan People and Institutions,* Calcutta, 1969, p. 3ff.

(h) Kosambi, Damodar Dharamanand: *An Introduction to the Study of Indian History,* Bombay, 1991 (reprinted), pp. 81, 94-5.

4. (a) Mukherjee, Prabhati: *Beyond the Four Varnas, The Untouchables in India,* Delhi 1988, p. 17ff.

(b) Srivastava, Suresh Narain: *op. cit.,* pp. 3, 16.

(c) Ghurye, G.S.: *Caste and Race in India,* Bombay, 1979 (5th edn), p. 75ff.

(d) Dutt, N.K.: *Origin and Growth of Caste in India,* Calcutta, 1986, p. 25ff.

(e) Bhattacharyya, N.N.: *Ancient Indian History and Civilization, Trends and Perspectives,* New Delhi, 1988, p.143ff.

5. (a) Ambedkar, B.R.: "Who were the Shudras?" in *Dr. Babasaheb Ambedkar, Writings and Speechs,* Vol. 7, Bombay, 1990, pp. 65-100.

(b) Rao, R. Sangeetha: *Caste System in India,* New Delhi, 1989, p. 23ff.

(c) Elst, Koenraad: *Indigenous Indians—Agastya to Ambedkar,* New Delhi, 1993, pp. 59-60, 162-3.

(d) Rajaram Navaratna S.: *Aryan Invasion of India,* New Delhi, 1993, pp. 56, 57.

(e) Talageri, Shrikant G.: *Aryan Invasion Theory and Indian Nationalism,* New Delhi, 1993, pp. 64, 65.

(f) Sethna, K.D.: *The Problem of Aryan Origins,* New Delhi, 1992 (Enlarged Edition), p. 83.

Note: There are other scholars, M.M. Ganganath Jha, D.S. Trivedi, L.D. Kalla, who uphold the theory of the indigenous origin of the Aryans. These scholars' views are summed up in an appendix in *The History and Culture of the Indian People, The Vedic Age,* London, 1951, pp. 215-17.

6. (a) Phule, Jotirao Govindrao: "Slavery" in *Collected Works of Mahatma Jotirao Phule,* Vol. I, Bombay, 1991, p. xxix (Preface).

(b) Ghosh B.K.: *op.cit.,* pp. 201-12.

(c) Srivastava, Suresh Narain: *op. cit.,* pp. 1-3.

(d) Chanda, Ramaprasad: *op. cit.,* pp. 14-15.

(e) Chattopadhyaya, K.P.: p. 32ff.

(f) Fuchs, Stephen: *The Aboriginal Tribes of India,* London, 1977, p. 18ff.

(g) Hutton, J.H.: *Caste in India, Cambridge,* 1946, p. 5ff.

(h) Swami Dharma Theerth : *History of Hindu Imperialism,* Madras, 1992 (15th edn.), pp.13-23.

(i) Chatterji, Suniti Kumar: *Indo-Aryan and Hindi,* Calcutta, 1990, pp.1-30.

(j) Nehru, Jawaharlal: *The Discovery of India,* London, 1951, pp. 56, 57.

(k) Kosambi, D.D.: *The Culture and Civilisation of Ancient India in Historical Outline,* New Delhi, 1992 (reprint), p. 53.

(l) Kulke, Hermann and Dietmar Rothermund: *A History of India,* New Delhi, 1991 (Indian edition), p.19.

7. A summary of Dr. Ambedkar's views is found on page 242 in his work "The Untouchables, who were they and why they became Untouchables?" in *Babasaheb Ambedkar, Writings and Speeches,* Vol. 7, *op. cit.*
8. Rao, R. Sangeetha: *op. cit.,* p. 23ff.
9. Bhattacharrya, N.N.: *op. cit.,* p. 30ff.
10. Chanda, Ramprasad: o*p. cit.,* p. 3.
11. *Rigveda* 1.51.8.
Note: All the *Rigveda's* Sanskrit verses text is taken from *Rigveda* in Devanagri script edited by Shriram Sharma Acharya, published in four volumes by Sanskrit Sansthan, Bareilly (U.P.), 1985.
12. *Rigveda* 3.34.9.
13. *Rigveda* 1.7.9.
14. *Rigveda* 1.108.8.
15. *Rigveda* 6.20.12.
16. *Rigveda* 1.33.4.
17. *Rigveda* 10.22.8.
18. *Rigveda* 5.38.10.
19. *Rigveda* 1.103.3,4.
20. *Rigveda* 2.12.3.
21. *Rigveda* 2,20,7,8.
22. *Rigveda* 7.83.1.
23. *Rigveda* 10.38.3.
24. *Rigveda* 10.151.3.
25. *Rigveda* 10.157.4.
26. *Rigveda* 1.35.10.
27. *Rigveda* 6.51.14.
28. Macdonell, Arthur Anthony and Arthur Berriedall Keith (in future reference, Macdonell and Keith): *Vedic Index of Names and Subjects,* Vol. I, London, 1912, p. 64.
29. *Ibid.,* p. 347.
30. S.V. 'Arya' and 'Dasyu', Apte, Vaman Shivram: *op. cit.*, pp. 229, 494.
31. Macdonell and Keith: *op.cit.*, pp. 466-7.
32. Cf. Griffith, Ralph T.H.: *The Hymns of the Rigveda,* Delhi, 1986 (reprinted), p. 5 (footnote 9).
33. Chanda, Ramprasad: *op.cit.,* p.15.
34. *Rigveda* 1.32.6, 1.51.5; 2.146, 6.314 etc.
35. *Rigveda* 1.133.8, 7.5.3. etc.
36. *Dr. Babasaheb Ambedkar: Writings and Speeches,* Vol. 7, *op. cit.* pp. 86-100.
37. Griffith, Ralph T.H.: *op. cit.*, 342 (footnote 7).
38. Chattopadhyaya, K.P.: *op.cit.,* pp. 7, 8.
39. Possehl, Gregory L. (ed.): *Ancient Cities of the Indus,* New Delhi, 1979.
40. Mackay, Ernest (2nd edn. revised and enlarged by Dorothy Mackay): *Early Indus Civilization*, Patna, 1989 (reprinted).

41. Wheeler, Sir Mortimer: *The Cambridge History of India Supplementary Volume, The Indus Civilization*, Cambridge, 1953.
42. Marshall, Sir John: "Harappa and Mohenjodaro" in *Ancient Cities of the Indus, op. cit.*, p.181.
43. Gurdip Singh: "The Indus Valley Culture" in *Ancient Cities of the Indus, op. cit.*, p. 234.
44. Fairservis, Jr. Walter A.: "The Origin, Character and Decline of an Early Civilization" in *Ancient Cities of the Indus, op. cit.*, p. 79.
45. Mackay, Ernest: *op. cit.*, p. 10.
46. *Ibid.*, p. 77.
47. Sankalia, H.D.: "The 'Cemetery H' Culture" in *Ancient Cities of the Indus, op. cit.*, p. 324
48. Dales, George F.: "The Mythical Massacre at Mohen-jodaro" in *Ancient Cities of the Indus, op. cit.*, p. 296
49. Wheeler, Sir Mortimer: *op. cit.*, p. 86.
50. Mackay, Ernest: *op. cit.*, p. 148.
51. *Ibid.*, pp. 13, 14.
52. Dales, George F.: "New Investigations at Mohenjo-daro" in *Ancient Cities of the Indus, op. cit.*, p. 194.
53. Dales, George F.: "The Decline of the Harappans" in *Ancient Cities of the Indus, op. cit.*, p. 311.
54. Kramer, Samuel N.: "The Indus Civilization and Dilmun: The Sumerian Paradise Land" in *Ancient Cities of the Indus, op. cit.*, pp. 168-9.
55. Wheeler, Sir Mortimer: *op. cit.*, p. 2.
56. See Kapur Singh: *op. cit.*, pp. 170, 171.
57. Wheeler, Sir Mortimer: *op. cit.*, p. 51.
58. Mackay, Ernest: *op. cit.*, p. 4.
59. See for details and more views about the date:
    a) Samuel N. Kramer: *op. cit.*, p. 171.
    b) Thapar, B.K.: "Kalibangan: A Harappan Metropolis the Indus Valley" in *Ancient Cities of the Indus, op. cit.*, p. 202.
    c) Gurdip Singh: *op. cit.*, p. 235.
    d) Zide, Arlene R.K.: "A Brief Survey of Work to Date on the Indus Script" in *Ancient Cities of the Indus, op. cit.*, p. 257.
    e) Raikes, Robert L: "The End of the Ancient Cities of the Indus" in *Ancient Cities of the Indus, op. cit.*, p. 297.
60. See for detailed analysis:
    a) Kapur Singh: *op. cit.*, pp. 146-7.
    b) Mackay, Ernest: *op. cit.*, p. 4.
61. Mackay, Ernest: *op. cit.*, p. 157.
62. See Kapur Singh: *op. cit.*, p. 227.
    Wheeler, Sir Mortimer: *op. cit.*, pp. 91, 92.
63. See Raikes, Robert L.: *op. cit.*, p. 301.
64. Gurdip Singh: *op. cit.*, p. 242.

65. Fairservis, Jr., Walter A.: "The Harappan Civilization: New Evidence and More Theory", in *Ancient Cities of the Indus, op. cit.,* p. 50.
66. Battacharyya, K.P.: *op. cit.,* pp.1-26.
67. Majumdar, R.C. and A.D. Pusalkar (eds.): *op. cit.*, pp. 123-200.
68. Chattopadhyaya, K.P.: *op. cit.,* pp. 43-46.
69. Wheeler, Sir Mortimer: *op. cit.,* pp. 18, 90-2.
70. Zide, Arlene R.K.: *op. cit.,* pp. 256-60.
71. Bhattacharyya, N.N.: *op. cit.,* p. 23.
72. Zide, Arlene R.K.: *op. cit.,* p. 257.
73. Wheeler, Sir Mortimer: *op. cit.,* p. 18.
74. *Ibid.,* pp. 90-3.
75. Pusalkar, A.D.: "The Indus Valley Civilization" in *The Vedic Age, op. cit.*, p. 179.
76. Chattopadhyaya, K.P.: *op. cit.*, p. 44.
77. (a) Quoted in *The Land of the Five Rivers* by Hugh Kennedy Trevaskis, Oxford, 1928, p. 21.
    Also see:
    (b) Desikachar, S.V.: *Caste, Religion and Country,* New Delhi, 1993. p. 116.
78. (a) Chanda, Ramprasad: *op. cit.,* p. 3.
    (b) Mukherjee, Prabhati: *op. cit.,* pp. 78, 79.
    (c) Thapar, Romila: *From Lineage to State,* Bombay, 1990, p. 42.
79. Picket, J. Waskom: *Christian Mass Movements in India*, New York, 1933, p. 217.
80. Griffith, Ralph T.H.: *The Hymns of the Rigveda*, Delhi, 1986 (reprinted), p. 603.
81. Dutt, N.K.: *op. cit.,* p. 25.
82. Fr. Zacharias: *An Outline of Hinduism,* Alwaye, 1956, pp.21 and 117.
83. Hume, Robert Ernest (tr): *The Thirteen Principal Upanishads,* London, 1951 (reprinted), p. 233.
84. Fr. Zacharias: *op. cit.,* p. 360.
85. *Ibid.*, pp. 375, 376.
86. Sen, Makhan Lal (tr.): *Ramayana,* Calcutta, 1989, pp. 699-702.
87. Goyandaka, Jayadyal (ed.): *Snkhipat Mahabhrate* (Hindi), Gorakhpur, n.d., pp. 69-72.
88. Swami Vireswarananda (tr.): *Srimad Bhagvad-Gita,* Madras, 1987, p. 128.
89. *Ibid.,* pp. 506-8.
90. *Ibid.,* p. 282.
91. Burnell Arthur Coke (tr.): *The Ordinances of Manu,* New Delhi, 1971, p. xxiii (Introduction).
    Also see Fr. Zacharias: *op. cit.*, p. 323.
92. *Ibid., p.* 305.
93. See for discussion on "Anuloma'"and "Pratiloma":
    Srivastava Suresh Narain: *op. cit.,* pp. 25-8.

94. Burnell, Arthur Coke (tr.): *op. cit.,* p. 306 (*Manusmriti* 10.12). p. 310 (*Manusmriti* 10.38).
95. *Ibid.,* p. 312 (*Manusmriti* 10.51, 52).
96. See for detailed discussion:
(a) Rao, R. Sangeetha: *op. cit.,* pp. 72-80.
(b) Ghurye, G.S.: *op. cit.,* pp. 69-72.
97. Quoted in Forrester, Duncan B.: *Caste and Christianity,* London, 1980, p. 11.
98. Ghurye, G.S.: *op. cit.*, p. 71.
99. Quoted in Forrester, Duncan B.: *op. cit.,* p. 11.
100. Banks, Marcus: *Organizing Jainism in India and England,* Oxford, 1992, p.27.
101. *Ibid.,* p. 52.
102. Ambedkar, Dr. B.R.: "The Untouchable", *op. cit.*, p. 315.
103. Narasu, P. Lakshmi: *The Essence of Buddhism,* Bombay, 1948, p. 98.
104. Zelliot, Eleanor: "The Psychological Dimension of the Buddhist Movement in India" in G.A. Oddie (ed.), *Religion in South Asia—Religious Conversion and Revival Movements in South Asia in Medieval and Modern Times*, New Delhi, 1991, p. 204.
105. See for detail of facts and dates in:
Francis Watson: *A Concise History of India*, Southampton. 1981 (reprinted), pp. 87-124.
106. Ahmad, Imtiaz (ed.): *Caste and Social Stratification among Muslims in India,* New Delhi, 1978, p. 14.
107. Al-Biruni: *India* (abridged edition of Dr. Edward C. Sachau's English translation and edited by Qeyamuddin Ahmed, New Delhi, 1988 (revised), p. 46.
108. See for detailed discussion:
(a) Dumont, Louis: *Homo Hierarchicus, The Caste System and its Implications,* Chicago, 1970, pp. 205-12.
(b) Mandelbaum, David G.: *Society in India,* Bombay, 1990 (reprinted), pp. 246-51.
109. Grewal, J.S.: *Guru Nanak in History,* Chandigarh, 1979 (reprinted), p. 61.
110. *Ibid.,* p. 40.
111. Ahmed, Imtiaz (ed.): *op. cit.*, 1973, pp. xxx-xxxi (Introduction).
112. Mandelbaum, David G.: *op. cit.,* pp. 560-1.
113. Weil, Shalva: "Symmetry between Christians and Jews in India: The Cananite Christians and the Cochin Jews of Kerala", *Indian Sociology,* 16/2, Paris, 1992, pp. 194-5.
114. Mandelbaum, David G.: *op. cit.,* p. 563.
115. On December 3, 1993, the author visited in Cochin the locality known as Kochi (Jew Town) and visited the local synagogue. He asked a number of questions of local Jews and others. He was told that there is even a separate worship place for the *Kala* (black) Jews, and there are very little social

dealings between two groups.

116. Weil, Shalva: *op. cit.,* p. 184.
117. Kulke, Eckehard: *The Parsees in India,* New Delhi, 1993 (reprint), pp. 13, 26.
118. *Ibid.,* p. 48.
119. a) Boman-Behram B.K.: "Social Relationship between the Communities", in Nancy and Ram Singh (eds.), *The Sugar in the Milk–The Parsis in India,* Delhi, 1986, pp. 53-4.
     b) Kulke, Eckehard: *op. cit.*, p. 28.
120. Singh, Ram: "The Incredible Community", in *The Sugar in the Milk, op. cit.,* p. 3.
121. Mandelbaum, David G.: *op. cit.*, p. 537.
122. Marenco, Ethne K.: *The Transformation of Sikh Society,* New Delhi, 1976, pp. 26, 298.
123. Majumdar, R.C.: "Evaluation of Religio-Philosophic Culture in India", in Haridas Bhattacharyya (ed.), *The Cultural Heritage of India, Volume IV, The Religions,* Calcutta, 1983 (reprint), p. 61.
124. Marenco, Ethne K.: *op. cit.*, pp. 41-2.
125. *Ibid.,* p. 63.
126. *Ibid.,* p. 285.
127. Garlington, W.: "The Baha'i Faith in Malwa", in G.A. Oddie (ed.), *Religion in South Asia,* New Delhi, 1991, (2nd rev. & and enlarged edn.), p. 181.
128. *Ibid.,* p. 182.
129. Kaye, John William: *Christianity in India,* London, 1959, p. 38.
130. Watson, Francis: *op. cit.,* p. 125.
131. *Ibid.,* pp.141-4.
     Also see: *The Untouchable Story,* by D.P. Das, New Delhi, 1985, p. 171.
132. Galanter, Marc: *Competing Equalities in Law and the Backward Classes in Media,* Delhi, 1984, p. 19.
133. Kay, John William: *op. cit.,* p. 375.
134. See for detailed discussion: *Religion and Society*, XXXVI, 4, December 1989, pp. 26-8.
135. Kay, John William: *op. cit.,* pp. 30-3, 352-3.
136. See for details: Rao, R. Sangeetha: *op. cit.,* p. 106-16.
137. Srivastava, Suresh Narain: *op. cit.*, pp. 247-8.
138. *Dr. Babasaheb Ambedkar, Writings and Speeches,* Vol.7, *op.cit.*,p. 4.
139. Ghurye, G.S.: *op. cit.,* pp. 286-7.
140. Lokhande, G.S.: *Bhimrao Ramji Ambedkar,* New Delhi, 1982, p. 9.
141. Vakil, A.K: *Gandhi–Ambedkar,* New Delhi, 1982, p. 47.
142. See for summary of these movements and their work:
     Ouwerkerk, Louise: *The Untouchables of India,* Oxford, 1945, pp. 16-29.
143. Lokhande, G.S.: *op. cit.,* p. 181.
144. Hutton, J.H., *op. cit.*, p. 167.

145. Ghurye, G.S.: *op. cit.*, p. 306.
146. Isaacs, Harold R.: *India's Ex-Untouchables,* 1965, Bombay, p. 36.
147. *Ibid.*, pp. 39-41.
148. See for detailed discussion: *Bulletin of the Christian Institute for Religious Studies*, 20/1, January 1991 pp. 3-6.
149. Rajasekhriah. A.M.: *B.R. Ambedkar -The Quest for Social Justice,* New Delhi, 1989, p. 63.
150. *Ibid.*, pp. 66-7.
Also See: Ouwerkerk, Louise: *op. cit.*, p. 42.
151. Baxi, Upendra: "Political Justice, Legislative, Reservation for Scheduled Castes and Social Change" (Dr. Ambedkar Memorial Lectures–1978), University of Madras, p. 9.
152. Zelliot, Eleanor: *op. cit.*, p. 188.
153. Gupta, S.K.: *The Scheduled Castes in Modern Indian Politics,* New Delhi, 1985, pp. 211-12.
154. *The Constitution of India: op. cit.*, p. 178.
155. *Ibid.*, p. 203.
156. See Galanter, Marc, *op. cit.*, p. 132.
157. *Indian Express,* New Delhi, June 13, 1990, p. 9.
158. Taken from the proposed text of 'The Constitution (Scheduled Castes) Orders (Amendment) Bill, 1990.
159. *The Constitution of India: op. cit.*, p. 176.
160. Shrikant, L.M.: *Report of the Commissioner for Scheduled Castes and Scheduled Tribes for the period ending 31st December, 1951*, p. 1.
161. *Ibid.*, p. 1.
162. *Ibid.*, p. 12.
163. *Report of the Commissioner for Scheduled Castes and Scheduled Tribes* (April 1985–March 1986). Eighth Report, Government of India, New Delhi, pp. 35-43.
164. *Ibid.*, p. 17.
165. Galanter, Marc: *op. cit.*, p. 1.
166. *Report of the Backward Classes Commission,* Government of India, First part, Volumes I & II, 1980, p.1.
167. *Ibid.*, p. 2.
168. *Ibid.*, pp. 5-11.
169. *Ibid.*, p. VII (introductory).
170. *Ibid.*, p. 14.
171. *Ibid.*, p. 16.
172. *Ibid.*, p. 48.
173. *Ibid.*, p. 20.
174. *Ibid.*, p. 14.
175. *Ibid.*, p. 21.
176. *Ibid.*, p. 22.
177. *Ibid.*

178. *Ibid.*
179. *Ibid.*
180. *Ibid.*
181. *Indian Express,* New Delhi, August, 18, 1991, p. 8.
182. Moses, Brindavan C: "New Delhi's Elite's Battle for Status quo", in *Defences of Mandal Commission, A Collection of Articles, Views and News,* Documentation by LEAS, Madras, n.d., pp. 33-4.
183. Omvedt, Gail: "Twice-Born", Riot Against Democracy, in *ibid.*, pp. 54-5.
184. Shrikant, L.M.: *op. cit.*, 1961, p. 2.
185. *Ibid.*, p. 9.
186. *Indigenous Peoples, a Global Quest for Justice,* a Report for the Independent Commission on International Humanitarian Issues—Foreword by Co-Chairman The Agha Khan and Hassan bin Talal, London, 1987, p. 6.
187. *Ibid.*, p. 7.
188. Quoted in *ibid.*, p. 8.
189. *Ibid.*, p. 10.
190. (a) Fuchs, Stephen: *op. cit.*, p. 25.
(b) Also see Fuchs' other work: *The Aboriginal Tribes of India,* London, 1983, p. 12f.
191. Trevaskis, Hugh Kennedy: *op. cit.*, p. 29.
192. Thapar, Romila: *op. cit.*, p. 28.
193. Mukherjee, Prabhati: *op. cit.*, pp. 28, 91.
194. Ghurye, G.S.: *op. cit.*, p. 52.
195. Dutt, N.K.: *op. cit.*, pp. 70, 71.
196. Ray, Niharranjan: Introductory Address, in K. Suresh Singh (ed.), *The Tribal Situation in India,* Shimla, 1986, reprinted. pp. 10, 11, 14 etc.
197. Griffith, Ralph T.H. (tr.): *op. cit.*, pp. 143, 220, 300, 322, 336.
198. Ambedkar, B.R.: *The Untouchables, op. cit.*, p. 241.
199. *Ibid.*, pp. 271-7.
200. *Ibid.*, p. 239.
201. Srivastava, Suresh Narain: *op. cit.*, p. 3.
202. *Ibid.*, pp. 9, 10.
203. Van Troy, J.: "Prehistory and Early History of Chotanagpur", in S. Bosu-Mullick (ed.), *Cultural Chotanagpur: Unity in Diversity,* New Delhi, 1991, pp. 34, 35.

CHAPTER TWO

Historical Background of the Christian Dalits

Problem of Christian Dalits as Christians

In the previous chapter it has been seen how the problem of today's Dalits started, how throughout history it developed systematically into its present state mainly through the sanction of religion, and also how the later religious movements were unable to play constructive roles in the problem of the Dalits. Histori-cally, Christian Dalits share common roots with the Dalits in general, but their case becomes special after they accept Christian religion. The Christian religion opposes any kind of discrimina-tion on the basis of race or sex or otherwise; it is supposed to be the most egalitarian faith. The *magna carta* of the Christian concept of equality is found in one of St. Paul's letters in these words: "There is no longer Jew or Greek, there is no longer slave or free, there is no longer male or female; for all of you are one in Christ Jesus."[1]

This egalitarian principle is possibly one that Christians in India have throughout ignored. This is one reason why the case of the Christian Dalits becomes special as compared to that of Dalits in general. As we have seen, by the Constitution (Scheduled Castes) Order, 1950, the Christian Dalits on the basis of religion have been deprived of their basic human rights including the consti-tutional fundamental rights, which the Constitution gives to other Dalits who profess Hinduism, Sikhism or Buddhism. Not only are they deprived of their basic rights of equality in Indian society, they are also equally deprived of their rights within the Christian Church or society. A great deal of evidence supporting this view is available from Christian and other sources. Some of these are cited below.

Both Roman Catholic and Protestant Church leaders have witnessed this problem openly. For example Archbishop George Zur, Apostolic Pro-Nuncio to India in his inaugural address to the Catholic Bishops Conference of India, (CBCI) at their meeting held in Pune during December 1991, made the following observations:

> Though Catholics of the lower castes and tribes form 60 per cent of Church membership they have no place in decision-making. Scheduled caste converts are treated as low caste not only by high caste Hindus but by high caste Christians too. In rural areas they cannot own or rent houses, however well-placed they may be. Separate places are marked out for them in the parish churches and burial grounds. Inter-caste marriages are frowned upon and caste tags are still appended to the Christian names of high caste people. Casteism is rampant among the clergy and the religious. Though Dalit Christians make 65 per cent of the 10 million Christians in the South, less then 4 per cent of the parishes are entrusted to Dalit priests. There are no Dalits among 13 Catholic bishops of Tamilnadu or among the Vicars-general and rectors of seminaries and directors of social assistance centres.[2]

The Pro-Nuncio's obsrvation was supported by Archbishop Alphonse Mathias, president of the CBCI. He added that the injustice meted out to Christian Dalits by the Government and the Church should be redressed fully.[3]

The Bishop in Madras of the Church of South India (a United Protestant Church) M. Azariah observes:

> The Scheduled Caste (Dalit) Christians are thus discriminated against and oppressed by fellow Christians within the various churches for no fault of their own but the accident of birth, even when they are 2nd, 3rd or 4th generation Christians. The high caste Christians who are in a minority in the Church carry their caste prejudices even after generations, unaffected by Christian belief and practice.[4]

Much earlier than these Christian sources, a number of scholars from other religions also argued the same point. For example B.R. Ambedkar (a Buddhist) not only raised this issue, he also made a commendable analysis why the Christian Dalits' negative status remained the same as before their conversion.[5] References will be made to his analysis at a later stage. Nirad C. Chaudhuri, the well known author and by faith a Hindu, also has pointed out the same reality in these words:

> All the Christian groups of India retain the mark of the caste system. They continue their caste status and pride of caste even in the generation born to Christianity and not merely converted to the new religion.[6]

Chaudhuri gave a number of examples including one of a Bengali Christian marriage, where an upper caste Christian opposed the idea of their son marrying the daughter of lower caste Christian parents.[7]

There is considerble evidence available from various Government-appointed commissions also. They have taken note of Christian Dalits' situation particularly in Kerala. For example, Kaka Kalelkar, chairman of the Backward Classes Commission in his letter to the Government of India on January 3, 1955 submitting the Commission's report, made the following observations:

> We discovered with deep pain and sorrow that untouchability did obtain in the extreme south among Indian Christians, and Indian Christians were prepared in many places to assert that they were still guided by caste, not only in the matter of untouchability, but in social hierarchy of high and low. While the harijans amongst the Hindus, classified as scheduled castes, stand a fair chance of bettering their conditions under the Indian Government's reservation policy, their Christian counterparts stand twice discriminated against.[8]

On this account Kaka Kalelkar referred to Christian Dalits as "twice discriminated." Twenty five years later the report of the second Commission of Backward Classes under the chairmanship of B.P. Mandal (detailed reference is made later on in Chapter Six) made a similar observation:

> Similar is the situation among Indian Christians... Christians in Kerala are divided... into various ethnic groups on the basis of their caste background ... even after conversion the lower caste converts continued to be treated as Harijans.... In the presence of rich Syrian Christians the Harijan Christians had to remove their headdress.... It was found that the Syrian and Pulaya members of the same church conduct religious rituals separately in separate buildings.... Thus lower caste converts to a very egalitarian religion like Christianity, ever anxious to expand its membership, even after generations were not able to efface the effect of their caste background.[9]

Why do the Dalits continue to suffer oppression and discrimination even after joining a very egalitarian religion like Christianity? The answer lies in the history of Indian Christians. Indian Christians, however, still do not have their own Indian Christian historiography. The most that is available are histories of various missions, not a history of the Indian Christians.[10] So this work has to depend upon scattered cases and information. First, a few cases of early missionaries are presented, and then some cases of early converts from the Dalit background. Next, an analysis is made of the problem of Christian Dalits. The purpose here is not to write a history of the Christian Dalits, but more to have a look at the available historical material, to see how far their history has contributed to the problems of Christian Dalits.

Indian Christian History

A lot of written material along with various analyses is now available on Dalit Christians.[11] Attempts are also being made to reconstruct the history of the Dalits (see Chapter One). One such recent attempt is *The Dalit Christians: A History* by John C.B. Webster.[12] It is a major attempt to present the case of the Christian Dalits. Webster, however, takes the nineteenth century as the starting point of Christian Dalit history.[13] whereas in the present work (Chapter One) the starting point of Christian Dalits history is taken from that moment of Indian history, when the Dalits problem in general started taking its shape, which on the basis of various literary as well as archaeological sources can be traced back to the "middle of the second millennium (1500 B.C.)".[14]

There are sufficient sources of information to show that Christian *contribution* to the problem of Christian Dalits started at a date much later than this, when Christian religion took root in Indian soil. Almost all Christian Church historians take pride in beginning Indian Christian history from the first century with the traditional claim that St. Thomas, one of the twelve disciples of Jesus Christ, came to Kerala then.[15] But it is also true that very little material is available in support of this thesis. Historically one can find enough evidence about the existence of Christian religion in Kerala from the fourth century with the coming of two emigrants, along with a trader named Thoma from Syria. From that point of history there existed a social distinction among the Syrian Christians. For example "Southist" Syrian Christians, who claim direct descent from Thoma of Canae, will not intermarry with "Northist" Syrian Christians.[16] One finds the roots of Christian Dalits getting deeper by the eighth century, when a local Hindu king granted a charter of 72 privileges to the head, Iravi Korttan of a later group of emigrants (see for more discussion Chapter One). About this Mathew and Thomas make the following observation:

> While such rights and privileges brought their own advantages to the Christian community, there was also a very unfortunate aspect of them, namely that the community, being thus recognised as high caste, came to look down upon the lower castes, and imbibed more or less the same attitude towards them as that of the high-caste Hindus.[17]

What these writers call the "unfortunate aspect" of the charter of privileges, was the starting point of the problem of the future Christians in Kerala from the Dalit background. The reports of the two Backward Classes Commissions (1955 and 1980), make it clear that this "unfortunate aspect" continues to dominate the life of Kerala Christians, because of which the Christian Dalits continue to suffer various disabilities in the Church.

What about Christian Dalits from other regions or states of India? To understand the historical background of their problem, a few important cases beginning with the arrival of the first western Roman Catholic missionary during the sixteenth century are studied below. We consider, first, important selected cases of western missionaries in South India and in North India and then a case from Panjab Church History.

Western Missionaries in South India

Both in South and North India, there was a similar prelude to the western missionaries' work. For example before the first Roman Catholic western missionary Francis Xavier, in 1497 arrived the first Portuguese trader Vasco da Gama in South India. The Syrian Christians welcomed him. On his second visit to South India, Vasco da Gama came with the title of Admiral of the Eastern Seas, from the King of Portugal. The Christians of South India (Malabar) welcomed him again and asked him to be their ruler. According to a western historian, from that time "a tyrannous, lustful, and unscrupulous" rule began. John William Kaye comments:

> But it is a painful and a terrible chapter of history. The first Christian settlers in India were the most un-Christian of men; and it has taken more than three centuries to wipe away the stain cast upon Christianity by the lives of its European professors.[18]

According to Kaye even the Franciscan friars who accompanied the Portuguese mariners to India were helpless in curbing the ungodly ways of the latter. They of course founded monasteries and built churches, but they failed to win even a few genuine converts. Again Kaye says:

> Proselytism, in the time of Albuquerque, was a matter of state

> policy, not of Christian zeal and devotion. The Viceroy, we are told, "in order to breed up soldiers, very wisely got the Indian maids made Christians and married them to the Portuguese, that they might not always stand in need of fresh supplies of men from Portugal."[19]

Kaye also remarks: "Maffeus candidly acknowledges that the unholy lives of the Portuguese formed one of the main obstacles to the conversion of the natives".[20] A little later it will be seen how similar was the work of western missionaries in North India. These painful parts of the Christian story in India are important, because they have a bearing upon the Christian Dalits.

Francis Xavier and Roberto de Nobili

The first western missionary was a Roman Catholic Jesuit Francis Xavier, who arrived in October 1542. He adopted a simple method of preaching. He translated the Apostles' Creed, the Lord's Prayer and the Ten Commandments into Tamil. Then he took a bell in his hand, and went ringing it, first in the streets of Goa and then village to village on the western coast among the fishermen. It is believed he baptised 700,000 people belonging to different caste groups, but the majority of his converts came from *pariah* people (outcaste). Francis Xavier went to other places also. He died on December 2, 1552.[21]

The next well-known missionary who played an important, though negative role in the history of the Christian Dalits was a Jesuit missionary named Roberto de Nobili. He arrived in Madurai (South India) in A.D. 1606. He found that the Christian religion had succeeded only among the low castes. This was because the Portuguese, who were known as *pharangis*, ate beef, drank liquor, seldom bathed and mingled with the lower caste people. Therefore, Kaye says

> Rejecting the example of Xavier, whose warm heart had expanded towards the poor and the oppressed, and whose ready limbs had ever borne him amongst them, Robert de Nobilibus, his associates, and his successors, addressed

> themselves to the dominant class, and sought their converts among the Brahmans.[22]

In order to gain converts from the upper castes Roberto de Nobili declared himself a high-caste *raja* (king). He said he was not a *pharangi,* but a royal person from Rome. Later on he, along with his colleagues, declared that they were "new Brahmans" (priests). They even forged a Sanskrit document proving that they sprang from the head of Brahma (god of creation) himself. The tradition of that time was that the original *Vedas* had been lost. Roberto de Nobili declared that he had found the lost *Veda* and he was teaching from that. He accepted strictly vegetarian food, Indian clothes of a priest and started following all the Hindu religious customs. He accepted caste and practised untouchability. The result of de Nobili's tactics was that many upper caste Hindus became Christians.[23]

Roberto de Nobili also introduced separate missionary priests for upper-caste Christians and low caste Christians, calling them *Brahman sanyasis* and *Pandara swamis* respectively.[24] Ultimately the efforts of de Nobili and his associates brought fruit, which for the future proved negative: a divided Church was created. By their actions they perpetuated "the distinctions which it is the ambition of Christianity to destroy. The high-caste Christians and low caste Christians were suffered to worship apart. They could not pray in the same temple. They could not dip their fingers in the same holy water."[25] Kaye makes an interesting remark about the overall work of Roberto de Nobili and his associates. He says:

> That these Jesuits made a surprising number of converts in the south....They baptised many thousands of people, the record is doubtless true. If the sprinkling of water and the utterance of a certain formula be enough to make a Christian, as many professing Protestants seem to believe, even in the middle of the seventeenth century, doubtless made multitudes of Christians. According, however, to their own showing, their success among the Brahmans was very small, and they soon began to see the necessity of flying at lower game.[26]

Kaye further says in this regard that these Jesuits "went among the people with great parade of caste, and declared that they had sprung from the head of Brahma (creator god) himself".[27]

Ziegenbalg and Plutschau

Ziegenbalg and Plutschau were the first Protestant missionaries in India. They studied at the University of Halle, a great centre of evangelical Christianity, under the learned and pious Professor Francke.[28] Theologically they were both trained in the tradition of pietism which was highly individualistic.[29] The pietistic traditions in which they were trained had stressed the second or new birth. Professor Francke himself had a dramatic conversion experience in 1686.[30] On arrival at Tranquebar in 1706 Ziegenbalg and Plutschau first mastered the local language and started translating the Scripture. Their method of preaching was different from that of Jesuits; it was a set of moral oral teachings and a mere ceremony of baptism. But as per the pietistic tradition, Ziegenbalg and his colleagues' work was based on the Bible. Therefore they provided the scripture as basis for their teaching. Their first convert, who was a poor slave (lower caste), was baptised on May 12, 1707. Their later converts were also mostly from the lower poor castes. It was painful for them to know that "Christianity... in the understanding of the natives of the country was only a synonym for ruin".[31]

Besides Ziegenbalg and Plutschau another important early Lutheran missionary was Christian Frederick Schwartz, who was also trained at the University of Halle. Schwartz did help the poor people, but it was for him a secular work. He considered this kind of work subordinate to spiritual work.[32]

Western Missionaries in Eastern India

Already references have been made to the un-Christian life of early Christian settlers, who were mainly Portuguese. Many of them according to C.F. Andrews were later on settled among small groups of English people on the banks of river Hooghly in Bengal. About their historical background C.F. Andrews says:

> The first field of missionary endeavour is interesting and typical of the age. The Portuguese had for many years carried on a slave trade along the coast of India. Those who were kidnapped were frequently baptized and called by Portuguese names. Their descendants gained their freedom, but remained utterly ignorant of Christianity, living the most degraded lives. At one time the evil of this practice of baptizing those who had been kidnapped, grew so great that the Mahars Government was obliged to pass a law upon the subject preventing the baptism of slaves. A considerable number of Indians of this type, who went by the name of "Portuguese" were settled among the tiny body of English settlers on the banks of the Hughly, in Bengal.[33]

In this area the first Protestant missionary of the English Church, J. Kiernander, began his work on the invitation of Lord Clive in 1758. Kiernander also was educated at the University of Halle under the son of Professor Francke, the teacher of Ziegenbalg and Plutschau. Kiernander had come to South India in 1740.[34] He served in Calcutta for 40 years without learning the local language Bengali. His work was carried on in a corrupt form of Portuguese. His congregation, according to C.F. Andrews, included "Jews, Chinese, Armenians, Portuguese and Dutch, as well as small groups of Hindu converts, one of whom was a Brahman".[35] According to C.F. Andrews, Kiernander's period till his death at the close of the eighteenth century was one of the worst periods of Indian Church history. He says:

> During the closing decade of the eighteenth century the rule of the East India Company reached its lowest ebb. Moral interests and the welfare of the people were sacrificed to trade profits. Bengal was almost left to itself so far as the Church was concerned...We read constantly of Hindu idolatry being openly countenanced and even practised by officials who married Hindu wives and lived as petty rajahs... Professor Seeley has named this time the "brahmanizing" period of English rule. Divorced from Christian influence and sharing in the evils of the idolatry around, English life became unspeakably corrupt.[36]

The famous Baptist missionary William Carey along with his associates began his work in Calcutta in 1793, which was followed with an appointment of the first Bishop of the Church of England, Bishop Middleton, in 1814 and his successor Bishop Heber in 1823. In 1830 a well known Presbyterian missionary, Alexander Duff, also began his work in Calcutta. The work of these pioneer missionaries in a way laid down the future of the Christian community in North India and also had a direct bearing upon the Christian Dalits in the Church of the future.

Carey and Duff

William Carey came to Calcutta on November 11, 1793 accompanied by a colleague named Thomas. Later in October 1799, he was joined by other well-known Baptist missionaries William Ward and Joshua Marshaman.[37] Carey and his colleagues were disallowed trom working in the British territory in Calcutta, and hence went to Serampore, a territory ruled by the Danish King.[38] The purpose of his mission Carey explained in his little but famous work, which he wrote before coming to India in 1792 under the title "An Enquiry into the Obligations of Christians to use means for the conversion of the Heathen". The Indian heathen for Carey were "barbarous" and they had "savage manners". India, the country of "the barbarous Britons" was "the uncivilised state of the heathens".[39] To deal with his presumed state of Indians, Carey tried to use indigenous methods. About his missionary method John Webster Grant has observed:

> The core of Carey's strategy was the establishment of permanent centres of Christian work comparable in function to monasteries from which Europe was first Christianised. The mission compound was to be the cell from which the church would grow. From it evangelists would go out into neighbouring areas. Witnesses would be established in a variety of auxiliaries to Christian preaching, a school, a centre of study, a printing press to supply evangelists with Bibles and tracts... As part of their programme for reading the Indian mind Carey and his associates undertook serious study of Indian

> llterature, including the ancient sacred scripture... To the generation of missionaries that followed the Serampore group, however, progress seemed depressingly slow. A few of low caste were converted, but the Indian mind remained closed.[40]

Alexander Duff, whom the city of Calcutta received on May 27, 1830, was a Scottish Presbyterian.[41] Duff's way of working was opposite of Carey's. Whereas Carey was in favour of working in local languages and context, Duff gave preference to his own language English. According to him English language and culture combined with Christian teachings were the answer to all the problems of India. On his arrival he met another Englishman Charles Trevelyan. In their first meeting what took place Duff's biographer describes in the following words, which also reveals the overall purpose of Duff's mission. He says:

> In their first interview the two young men soon found themselves absorbed in this question above all others—the advantage, the positive necessity of using the English language as the medium of all Christianising and civilising, all high educational and administrative efforts by its rulers to reach the natural aristocracy and leaders of the people and through them to feed the vernaculars and raise the masses.[42]

The important expression to be noted is of course "English language as the medium of all Christianising and civilising". Carey and other early missionaries wanted to do the same through local languages, but Duff had his own reasoning and faith. His belief was not confined to the use of English language; he even believed the British administration could be used for the same purpose. His biographer comments:

> What the Christian Reformation did for Europe through the Greek tongue, the Roman law and the Bible in the vernaculars, it will similarly do for India and further Asia through the English language and the British administration.[43]

Duff also believed that through reaching "the natural aristocracy and leaders of the people (upper castes)", he would be able to "raise the masses". In a way similar to what Roberto de Nobili tried to do in South India by adopting a Brahmanical life-style, Duff tried through the adoption of western education and culture.

With these views before him, Duff "established in 1830 an English college for Indian students in which the highest culture and the science of the West should be taught in a Christian setting".[44] But such efforts—the use of English language and institutions, where it would be used as medicine, in Duff's own words, would be for "the selected youth of India".[45] John Webster Grant rightly has made a comparison with Duff's predecessor, when he says: "Unlike the elementary schools of Carey's tradition, the Christian colleges catered chiefly not to the children of converts, but to Hindus of the upper classes." These efforts of Duff brought fruit in the form of some baptisms[46] from upper castes, but how far Duff really succeeded in his approach we shall see a little later.

Middleton and Heber

In 1813 the British Government passed a bill, which gave more concessions and greater liberty to Christian missions. Earlier, it was also decided to establish an Indian bishopric. From a Cambridge background the first bishop elected was Thomas Fanshaw Middleton. Bishop Middleton started for India, as Kaye states: "fitted up (with) a library in his cabin furnished with more than a hundred volumes, Hebrew, Greek, Persian, Latin, French, and English–theological, classical, mathematical, historical and poetical".[47] He arrived in India on November 28, 1814. C.F. Andrews says of him:

> ...his tastes were academic and unpractical, and confined to a narrow circle of interests. When the Church in Calcutta needed a spiritual revival, the Church in South India was developing caste congregations, he was spending months of valuable time in wranglings as to privileges and official status. He regarded himself first and foremost as a government servant; ...he remained obdurate to the last in his refusal to ordain any Indian Christian to the sacred ministry.[48]

Middleton's successor, Bishop Heber, who reached India in October 1823, had a mind of his own. For example he ordained Abdul Masih on November 25, 1825, the first Indian Christian to be ordained by an Anglican Bishop.[49] Bishop Heber also applied his mind to the question of caste in the Church. Before his visit to the south in 1826, he wanted to prepare himself to face this question. He knew that even the famous missionaries Ziegenbalg, Schwartz and Gericke had accommodated the evil of caste in the Church. At that time there was a convert in Bishop's College by name Christian David, who was a follower of the doctrine and the practice preached by Christian Schwartz. Bishop Heber asked his opinion, who gave it in writing. Kaye has summarised Christian David's views in these words:

> First, with regard to nature of caste, it was declared by Christian David, that it was among the natives of Southern India, "purely a worldly idea"...From the days of Ziegenbalg downwards they had been warned to sit at church in two separate divisions, and had communicated separately at the Lord's table, drinking out of the same cup, but high-caste converts drinking first. As a proof, however, that was regarded as merely worldly distinctions, Christian David said that high-caste and low caste converts, among Christian congregations of the south, were buried in a common burial ground, took part promiscuously in the funeral ceremonies, "as if with the consciousness, contrary to the heathen nations, that death levelled all distinctions."[50]

Christian David, thus, considered that caste distinction was purely a worldly matter, of no great concern to Christianity as a religion. More significant in his view was the stage when one reached the grave in order to go to the other world; according to him this was the reason why all Christians were buried in a common graveyard. Ultimately Bishop Heber also accepted these views of Christian David, which in fact were the views of early missionaries such as Christian Schwartz. Bishop Heber concluded that in some form distinctions among all existed even in Europe and argued in these words:

> It may be called caste in one part of the world; it may be called blood, or anything in another; but in its essential feature the one thing differs little from the other. It is an intelligible and appreciable Christian principle that all men in the sight of God are equal. But it is equally certain that all are not equal in the sight of Man; and it is a fair presumption that God never intended them to be equal. Social distinctions exist everywhere; and if, argued the Bishop, the distinctions which exist among the converts on the Southern coast are merely social distinctions, why should we endanger the success of our efforts by endeavouring to enforce a law of equality, which is maintained among no other classes of men?[51]

A Case from Panjab Church History

The Presbyterian Church of the United States of America (known as A.P. Mission) began its work in the Panjab on November 5, 1834 with the arrival of its first missionary John C. Lowrie in Ludhiana, Panjab;[52] and the work of the United Presbyterian Church of America began on August 8, 1855 with the arrival of its first missionary Andrew Gordon in Sialkot, Panjab.[53] Interestingly, in these Presbyterian missions beginning from 1834, there were only 477 communicant members in 1885.[54] But thereafter, the number increased by thousands. The number of Christians belonging to all missions increased in the same way. In 1881, Christians in the Panjab numbered 3,796; in 1901 they were 37,980; and in 1921 this number went up to 375,031.[55] How did this happen? Andrew Gordon himself tells the story.[56]

The story began when a Hindu of the Jat caste (a Panjabi upper caste) by name Nattu was baptised on November 17, 1872 by the Rev. J.S. Barr. Not only was Nattu from a high caste, he was also son of a *lambardar* (village headman), and legal heir to his father's property and position. The missionaries were very happy at his conversion, but later on they were unhappy, because Nattu was disinherited. For them he proved a failure, "a weak brother". But this was not true, because he was instrumental in bringing into the Christian fold a person named Ditt, who later became instrumental in expanding the Church movement in the Panjab.

Ditt was from a village Shahabdike, which was about two miles from a larger village named Mirali, and thirty miles from Sialkot (now in Pakistan). Ditt was born around 1843. He was, to Gordon's description, "a man of the low and much despised Chura tribe ... a dark man, lame of one leg, quiet and modest in his manners, with sincerity and earnestness, well expressed in his face, and at that time about thirty years of age".[57] By profession Ditt was a hides dealer. He came into contact with Nattu, who taught him about Jesus Christ and in June 1873 Nattu took him to Sialkot for baptism.

The Rev. S. Martin was hesitant to accept Ditt for baptism. After all, his Christian teachings were based on the teaching of a "weak brother" Nattu. But Ditt's knowledge of Christianity was quite sound. He also looked up to Martin, an honest person. Still Martin wanted to delay his baptism, but Ditt was not willing to wait. In the words of Gordon: "Mr. Martin finally decided to baptize Ditt, not because he saw his way decidedly clear to do so, but rather because he could see no scriptural ground for refusing."[58]

Martin faced another problem. Immediately after baptism, Ditt asked permission to go back to his village. This was a new thing for Martin. The practice was that a new convert stayed with the missionary for more instruction and protection. Martin's worry was how this poor illiterate man would face opposition. Anyway Ditt returned to his village and this action of his proved the starting point for a Christian movement among the Churas (lowest sweeper caste/ outcaste) of the Panjab.[59]

On reaching home, Ditt did face bitter opposition from his relatives. A fellow villager taunted him: "Oh Ho! You have become a Sahib" (gentleman). Others said: "You have become a *be-i-man*" (one without religion). His sister-in-law said: "Alas, my brother, you have changed your religion without even asking our counsel; our relationship with you is over. Henceforth you shall neither eat, drink, nor in any way associate with us. One of your legs is broken already, so may it be with the other."[60]

But Ditt stood firm. He witnessed to his new faith in Christ openly and boldly both to his family members and others. The result was amazing. Three months after his baptism in August

1873, he had the privilege of taking his wife, his daughter and two neighbours to Sialkot for baptism. They walked thirty miles to be able to meet the missionaries. Martin examined them and was fully satisfied and gave them baptism.

To buy hides, Ditt used to visit many villages. Wherever he went on business, he preached about Christ also. In the eleven years after his baptism (1873-84), he brought into the Christian faith more than five hundred persons from his caste. By 1900 half the people of his caste had accepted Christ and by 1915 almost all the Churas of Sialkot district became Christians.[61]

A similar Christian movement took place among the Mazhabi Sikhs (Sikh by change of religion) and outcaste sweepers (known as Lal Begis) in the United Provinces (present Uttar Pradesh, North India).[62] A Christian movement among the Madigas (outcaste hide dealers) of Andhra Pradesh (South India) began also in the same way and progressed under the leadership of Vongole Abraham in Ellore area and another Dalit leader Vankayya in Kistna District of Telugu area.[63]

Analysis

For convenience sake, an analysis is being made under two heads: (1) general observations and (2) special comments based on available works, especially of scholars belonging to faiths other than Christian.

General observations

The *first* point that becomes clear is that Christians of Dalit background in the Christian community/churches in India suffer threefold discrimination: *one* at the hands of members of the Indian society in general; *two,* from Government of India, when it denies them constitutional rights which it gives to the Dalits in general (ref. Presidential Order, 1950); and *three* from Christians of upper caste/class background. This last one has very clearly begun from the time of the first group of Syrian Christians when they entered the State of Kerala during the fourth century and later on from eighth century as confirmed by C.P. Mathew and M.M.

Thomas. This problem now has become more visible as confirmed by various commissions appointed by Government and it is continuing till date, both in Kerala and other parts of India.

The *second* general point is that during the early years European Christians, particularly the Portuguese on the western coast of Goa and the English in Calcutta, contributed to the negative side of the image of the Christian community directly, which continues to haunt them even now as a reminder from fellow Indians. How this early image of Christians was created an early visitor, Terry of the seventeenth century, describes in the following words:

> To consider what scandal there is brought upon the Christian religion by the looseness and remissness, by the exorbitances of many which come amongst them, who profess themselves Christians of whom I have often heard the natives, who live near the ports where our ships arrive say thus, in broken English, which they have gotten—"*Christian religion, devil religion; Christian much drunks; Christian much do wrong; much beat, much abuse other.*"[64]

What Terry describes about the image created of Christianity by early Europeans continues to prevail even today.

Thirdly, the European missionaries who started coming from the sixteenth century onward, instead of correcting the situation, caused more confusion by a "compromising" or "accommodating" policy towards certain local practices, particularly the caste system within the Church. One may today blame Roberto de Nobili for initiating this practice in the Roman Catholic Church, but once it got started, it was equally followed by the Protestant missionaries in general which included Ziegenbalg and Bishop Heber. This caste problem is continuing within the walls of the Church.

The *fourth* point is the method or approach which most of the early missionaries used to preach the Christian Gospel – from the top. Here again it was not only the Roman Catholic missionary de Nobili or Duff the Presbyterian, it included even the later missionaries. The American Presbyterian pioneer missionary Andrew Gordon admits this when he says, "I began with my eye upon the large towns and cities... I began with the educated classes and people of good social positions, but ended among the poor and lowly."[65] Again Robert Clark, writing about the early work of the Church Missionary Society (Anglican) writes about one of their missionaries: "In Batala near Amritsar, Mr. Baring has established his boarding school for the better classes of native Christian boys."[66] The same truth is confirmed by a Scottish Presbyterian missionary Youngson, that is, their preferential approach to the upper caste Hindus and Muslims.[67] This method or missionary approach or attitude towards the Christian Dalits, again has left a deep imprint upon the psyche of Indian Christian communities in general.

The *fifth* point is the early missionaries' religious understanding of the Christian faith. Interestingly, most of these early Protestant missionaries were products of the University of Halle representing the religious beliefs of Professor Francke, with emphasis on personal holiness, an individualistic approach, other-worldliness, preparing souls for a heavenly future, considering the works of this world or issues related to life in this world as of second priority. John C.B. Webster in one of his works has summarised the position of the Presbyterian missionaries, which he calls "the Princeton Theology" and which has its theological link with the University of Halle (which will be referred in the later discussion). He says:

> The Princeton Theology played an important role in establishing patterns of interraction between the Presbyterian missionaries and the people of India. Because this theology derived from an infallible scripture which provided the divine standard according to which all truth must be judged and which was therefore not open to criticism based on any human (i.e. non-Biblical) standards of truth, it allowed only one-way interaction. The missionaries who came to India as bearers of this truth had everything to teach and nothing of importance to learn; the Indians, as proponents of human system, were expected only to accept the missionaries' truth with repentance, faith and thanksgiving—or reject it to their eternal peril.[68]

The above theological position with regard to the Christian work in India was followed by almost all Christian missionaries of various traditions and till date the majority of the Indian Christians accept it as the only truth worth believing.

Sixth, the "superiority complex", which an average missionary carried with him may be noted. For example a famous missionary and bishop of the Church of South India, Leslie Newbigin, on his return to England after retirement admits and testifies, how from the very beginning in 1936, they were considered as "Sahib" (Lord).[69] Another missionary, C.F. Andrews agrees, and says, "The missionary is not only a Westerner, but a Sahib."[70] Andrews cites an example to make his point clear. Once in a city in North India, he was walking along with an Indian, discussing the Christian faith. Just then a Sahib drove by in a trap with a groom seated behind. The crowd scattered before him, and the policemen saluted smartly. "Look", said the Indian gentleman, "there is your Christianity driving along! That Sahib is the missionary of this place, and that is his position, and that is how he goes to his work."[71]

Related to "Sahibism" among the Western missionaries, the racial superiority complex of British rulers in India as rulers is also responsible for the unchanged condition of Christian Dalits in India. For example Nirad Chaudhuri has compared the Muslim rulers with the British rulers (as Christians) and those lower caste people who became Muslims, with those who were converted to Christianity. He says that from his experience in Bengal, he could see that Muslims belonging to lower castes could gain a higher status with their fellow Muslims, because the Muslim rulers did identify with all the Muslims, which not only gave a new faith to the lower caste Muslim, but also a new political status. He says that:

> ... under the British rule in India, on the other hand, the Christians remained as much a subject population as the Hindus. I have heard that even in the churches in the olden days, the Indian congregation could not sit with the Europeans. The consciousness of racial superiority on which British rule in India rested was not concealed by Christianity. On the contrary,

the British rulers felt happy if Christianity did not infuse arrogance into the converts from Hinduism, and they attached the greatest possible importance to the saying that blessed are the poor in spirit.[72]

Seventh, the missionaries took it for granted that if they could win over the upper castes or leaders of Indian society, they would win over everybody or many. Already reference has been made to the general education of Indian Christians, which was mainly for the children of the upper castes. The examples are given of Duff's working and Baring School, Batala. Alexander Duff was not even happy when vernacular schools were opened for children of the lower castes.[73]

Among the missionaries there were two groups. One group were interested in increasing the number from the lower castes for the sake of numbers; the other group were opposed to the whole idea of accepting converts from the lower castes. These groups among the missionaries existed from the very beginning, Francis Xavier representing the first group and Roberto de Nobili the second. Tyndale Biscoe (a missionary of the Church of England) in his autobiography speaks of how the first group used to baptise people at sight by filling "a bowl full of water and sprinkling on the person in front of the whole crowd would say: 'In the name of the Father, the Son and the Holy Ghost'."[74] Tyndale Biscoe also reports how a senior Methodist missionary rebuked a junior missionary for not maintaining increase of baptisms; he was afraid of losing dollars from America.[75]

The early missionaries as well as later ones created the myth that a convert belonging to high caste had to lose much from the worldly point of view, whereas a convert from a lower caste lost nothing. But it is not true.[76] The fact is that most of the high-caste converts almost always have gained much more than the lower castes, even from the worldly point of view. For example, the first Presbyterian convert's family, even today, own the largest property in Jullundur.[77] All these worldly means were developed with the help of the missionaries, but that cannot be said of the Christians from the lower castes; they only got odd jobs from the missionaries, such as gardener, cook, sweeper, and so on.[78]

The missionaries were uneasy with the low-caste converts. They referred to them only as "mass movement Christians" or simply Christians. The title "convert" they reserved only for the upper caste Christians.[79] Because of this distinction, some missionaries would not mention in their reports the caste of the lower caste Christians. They referred to them as "common villagers" or "illiterate menials."[80] One missionary, J.C.R. Ewing, while reporting to his Board of Foreign Missions of the USA referred to his performance in converting these lower caste Christians as "raking in rubbish into the Church".[81]

Again, missionaries as their common response to the caste problem, which may be labelled as "the policy of accommodation", divided the Indian Church or Indian Christians on the basis of their caste background. Even the Lord's Table was not spared, for they allowed the cup to be taken first by the upper caste Christians, and at the end by the lower caste.[82]

The missionary's response to the problem of Christian Dalits included establishing the "mission compounds", "Christian colonies" in the towns and cities, and for rural people "Christian villages". The main purpose of these settlements was to isolate these new Christians from the other people, who were considered to be heathen.[83] But this approach of the missionaries only helped in creating a distinctive but narrow Christian culture at the lower level.

Eighth, John Webster rightly says: "it was primarily the foreign missionaries rather than the Indian Christians who responded most eagerly to the Dalits' initiative."[84] But it is also true that it was mainly because of the Christian teaching they received, that they still remain in their old state. These Christian teachings failed to become part of their life. Christian David, referred to earlier, who declared that the caste problem is a "purely worldly idea", is a typical representative of the Indian Christians. He, of course, had absorbed the teachings and influence of his missionary master Christian Schwartz.

Ninth, the Indian Churches/Christians have further reinforced some of the unwelcome traditions followed by the missionaries. For example, the Christian educational institutions continue to strengthen the values of "upper ten" representing the oppressors.[85]

Tenth, the problems of the Christian Dalits have been exacerbated by a few Christians from the upper caste background. For example, at the time of making the Indian Constitution, the lower castes were given special economic privileges, free educa-tion for the children, special privileges with regard to government jobs and so on. A large majority of Christians had outcaste background and they were economically no better off than others of the same background belonging to other faiths. But the leaders representing these Christians in the Constituent Assembly were H.C. Mookerjee, a high caste Bengali convert; Amrit Kaur, a Panjabi convert from a royal background and Jerome D'Souza, S.J., a Jesuit. H.C. Mookerjee, said, as their spokesman, "I am a member of the minority community myself and a I feel proud that the community of which I am a member has decided to give up all special privileges..."[86] But this statement represented only the feeling and sentiments of the few upper caste Christians, not of millions of Christians having the Dalit background. Shankaranand Shastri goes further and says that some Christian leaders along with other minority leaders betrayed their communities by taking bribe. He says,

> After independence, in August 1947 the reservations for Muslims, the Christians, the Parsees, the Sikhs and Anglo-Indians were abolished... The Brahmins–Bania combination bribed the minority community leaders to surrender the reservations. Leaders like Maharaj Singh, a Christian leader and Modi, leader of Parsees were appointed governors of Bombay and U.P. to compensate the betrayal of their communities.[87]

Because of the stand that upper caste Christians took in the Constituent Assembly, as per the Order of the President of India, 1950 (amended in 1956 and 1990), the Indian Constitution does not give equal rights to Christian Dalits with other Indian Dalits in general.[88]

Special Comments

There are a number of analyses and comments, both critical and non-critical, made by scholars belonging to other faiths (Indian) and western Christian scholars and missionaries. Among the latter, reference has already been made to John William Kaye, C.F. Andrews, J. Waskom Picket, John Webster Grant, John C.B. Webster and Mark Juergensmeyer. Here, references are being made briefly to the analysis and comments offered by scholars belonging to other faiths, which include a historian N.N. Bhattacharyya, novelist Mulk Raj Anand, B.R. Ambedkar, and Nirad C. Chaudhuri.

N.N. Bhattacharyya

Regarding the attitude of early Christian missionaries towards the caste system he says:

> The Christian missionaries like De Nobili or Zeigenbalg believed that the caste system was a social institution of India totally unconnected with the basic principles of Hinduism, and as such there was no reason why a converted Christian should give up his caste identity, social position and traditional norms and customs. Hence for the propagation of Christianity not only did they make compromise with the caste system, but actively encouraged caste distinction even within the church, as a result of which caste feeling was more pronounced among the Christians of India, especially those of South India, than any other non-Hindu religious community.[89]

Bhattacharyya's comment call to mind Christian David, mentioned earlier. In response to Bishop Heber's enquiry, he confirmed that caste was "purely a worldly idea" and therefore from the days of Ziengenbalg there has been a practice "to sit at church in two separate divisions, and had communicated separately at the Lord's table, drinking out of the same cup, but the high-caste converts drinking first."[90]

Nirad C. Chaudhuri

Nirad C. Chaudhuri, in his work *The Continent of Circe* devotes a whole chapter to Indian Christians under the heading: "The Half-Caste Minorities: Genetic and Cultural". Chaudhuri divides Indian Christians, whom he describes as "half-caste", into two groups.

The first group are genetic, the result of marriages between Europeans and Indians, such as Anglo-Indians. The second (cultural) group of Christians are those who left their old religion and embraced the Christian faith. His focus is mainly on North Indian Christians, from Bengal to the Panjab.[91]

Chaudhuri's first comment is on the caste feeling among North Indian Christians. These caste differences may be seen in their social relationships like marriage and social functions. Being a Bengali, he has given an example from his own region.[92]

In the early days, Nirad Chaudhuri says, anyone who became a Christian was looked down upon by the Hindus, who believed in the genetic (through birth) principle for all human activities, including the religious. They regarded those who changed their religion as having done so out of fear or greed. On the other hand, British rulers in India, at least in the early period, used to think "that foreign rule could be maintained here only by respecting the beliefs, traditions and institutions of the native inhabitants".[93]

Chaudhuri points out: "There was not even equality between the official clergy in India, the members of the Ecclesiastical Establishment, and the missionaries, who were regarded as an inferior order. The Church of England, except in its missionary extension, never concerned itself with native souls."[94]

Chaudhuri acknowledges that in the beginning a number of converts came from the high caste Hindus who abhorred the gross idolatry and superstition of their own religion. But with the spread of education and stress on "a new form of Hindu monotheism", this tendency decreased.[95]

About the motivation of conversion of lower caste people he says:

> Those of them who wanted a rise in the social scale and better opportunities in life adopted Christianity, so that they might get not only equal treatment but also the protection of the ruling race through the missionaries of the same race....But the power of the caste system is such that the Hindus from the low castes who embraced Christianity did not raise themselves to a higher level, but on the contrary brought down the religion to their level.[96]

About the future of Indian Christians, Nirad's prophecy is also notable. He says:

> The wealthy and well-placed among them will become merged in the anglicised Hindu upper middle class, with only a difference of faith, which nobody including themselves will take very seriously. On the other hand the majority of Indian Christians, that is, those who are poor and already depressed socially, will become something like inferior caste in Hindu society.[97]

B.R. Ambedkar

B.R. Ambedkar has devoted two long essays to the subject, under the title "Christianising the Untouchables" and "The Condition of the Convert". He has referred extensively to both the history of Christian religion and its understanding by Christian missionaries. He has also pointed out clearly where they have gone wrong and why the conditions of the Christian Dalits are unchanged. On the aspect of history he has specially referred to the work of Roberto de Nobili,[98] Bishop Heber, Schwartz and Carey.[99] Explaining why in India theologically missionaries failed to make any impact upon the upper caste Hindus, he quotes a comment by Burn in the Census Report of 1901:

> To take a single concrete example, the ordinary educated Hindu laughs at the belief that God created the Universe out of nothing. He may believe in a creation, but he also postulates the necessity for both material cause, *matter* and an efficient cause, the *creator*. Whereas his belief is purely pantheistic, he also has no regard for historical evidence. A further difficulty on a fundamental point is caused by the belief in transmigration, which is based on the idea that a man must work out his own salvation and thus conflicts entirely with the belief in the Divine atonement.[100]

Commenting on this observation, Ambedkar said:

> Thus the Hindu speaks in terms of philosophy and the Christian speaks in terms of theology. There is thus no common ground for evaluation, or commendation or condemnation. In so far as both have theology the Christians with their God and Jesus as his son and the Hindus with their God and his Avatars, the superiority of one over the other depends upon the miracles performed by them. In this the Hindu theology can beat the Christian theology is obvious enough just as absence of philosophy in Christianity is responsible for its failure to attract the Brahmin and the educated Hindu. Secondly, the abundance of miracles in Hindu theology was enough to make Christian theology pale off in comparison.[101]

About the general condition of the Christian Dalits Ambedkar observes:

> It is necessary to bear in mind that Indian Christians are drawn chiefly from the Untouchables (Dalits) and, to a much less extent from low ranking Shudra castes. The social services of Missions must therefore be judged in the light of the needs of these classes. What are those needs? The services rendered by the Missions in the fields of education and medical relief are beyond the ken of the Indian Christians. They go mostly to benefit the high caste Hindu.[102]

This is true even today. The Jesuit Commission report in 1978 has also pointed out that the work of Roman Catholic Jesuits and "the Society's massive investment of men and resources in the educational apostolate in India..." have gone into propagating "the values of the 'upper ten'".[103] Ambedkar points out the two basic needs of Christian Dalits: "The first thing they want is the safeguarding of their civil liberties. The second thing they want is ways and means for their economic uplift."[104] He put a direct challenge to both the overseas missionary partners as well as to the Indian Christian Church leaders by saying:

> What has Christianity achieved in the way of changing the mentality of the convert? Has the Untouchable convert risen to status of the touchables? Have the touchable and untouchable converts discarded caste? Have they ceased to worship their old pagan gods and to adhere to their old pagan superstitions? These are far-reaching questions. They must be answered and Christianity in India must stand or fall by the answers it gives to these questions.[105]

Finally, Ambedkar also has given three main reasons why the Christian Dalits have failed to raise a movement, which could have led to change in their life and attitude. The *first* reason is a complete absence of desire on the part of the educated Christians, both upper castes and those from the Dalit background to take up the case of the community and fight for it. Because of this the Christian Dalits are still leaderless, and therefore they are unable to mobilise for the redress of their wrongs. *Second* is the mental make-up of the Christian Dalits, because of which they do not have a real urge to break from their past religious traditions. In a way their new Christian faith has become a kind of appendix to their old faith. The *third* reason is linked with the religious teachings of the Christian Church. When these Christian Dalits were Hindu, they were told that their negative Dalit state was due to *karma* (past deeds), but when they became Christians, they were told that their *dalitness* is because of the sins of their ancestors (original sin). Ambedkar adds: "In either case there is no escape for him."[106]

Mulk Raj Anand

Mulk Raj Anand's novel *Untouchable* was first published in 1935, when the controversy regarding Dalits in general between Gandhi and Ambedkar was at its climax. The text used here is from a revised edition reprinted in 1981. The novel's plot revolves round the life history of Bakha, who is eighteen years old, and his father Lakha, who is the head (*Jemadar*) of all the sweepers (Dalits). The novelist introduces Bakha in these words:

> Bakha had inherited from his forefathers: the weakness of the down-trodden (Dalit), the helplessness of the poor.[107]

While walking along a footpath Bakha touches by mistake an upper caste person. He is insulted and abused. Bakha is sad and angry. His father, hearing of this incident, reacts as follows:

> 'My son' said Lakha, with a forced mixture of anger and kindliness, 'didn't you give a warning of your approach?'
>
> 'But father, what is the use?' Bakha shouted. 'They would ill-treat us, even if we shouted. They think we are mere dirt, because we clean their dirt...'[108]

Lakha reminisces of an episode when Bakha was a child and was seriously ill. When Lakha went to a village doctor (*Hakim ji*) and entered his clinic, he was insulted and scolded by all upper caste persons present there who called him "Bhangi, Bhangi", meaning "sweeper." Hakimji himself called Lakha "Chandal" (the worst pejorative for a Dalit).

> 'He might have killed me', Bakha commented. 'No, no', said Lakha, 'they are really kind. We must realize that it is religion which prevents them from touching us.'[109]

Here the novelist comments:

> He (Lakha) had never throughout his narrative renounced his deep-rooted sense of inferiority and the docile acceptance of the laws of fate.[110]

This is how Mulk Raj Anand states the condition of his main characters, who are representative of the Dalit community in India and according to whom "religion" has been always behind the problem of the Dalits. To their problem of *dalitness,* three solutions were possible. One was "Jesus Christ", which was offered by a Christian missionary of the Salvation Army, Hutchinson. Second was "Gandhi", which was offered by Gandhi himself.

The third solution, offered by the novelist himself, is represented by machine (the flush system) which replaces the manual sweeping and cleaning.[111] According to the novelist, the first two options have failed. About the failure of Gandhi's method, he comments through the words of a strange character in his novel (a strange voice), which murmured in a crowd which went to welcome Gandhi:

> Gandhi is a humbug, it was saying 'He is a fool. He is a hypocrite. In one breath he says he wants to abolish untouchability, in the other he asserts that he is an orthodox Hindu. He is running contrary to the spirit of our age, which is democracy. He is in the fourth century B.C. with his swadeshi and his spinning-wheel. We live in the twentieth...'[112]

To Bakha's encounter with Colonel Hutchinson, the Salvation Army missionary, the novelist has devoted a number of pages. In one of the meetings Bakha was not looking well.

> 'What has happened? Are you ill?' The Colonel asked over... 'Nothing, Sahib, I was just tired,' said Bakha shyly. 'I am a sweeper here, son of Lakha, Jamadar of the sweepers'. 'I know, I know! How is your father?' 'Huzoor, he is well,' replied Bakha. 'Has your father told you who I am?' asked the Colonel, coming to the point in the practical manner of the English man. 'Han (yes), Huzoor (master). You are Sahib,' said Lakha, 'Nahin, nahin,' said the Colonel. 'I am not a sahib. I am like you. I am padre of the Salvation Army'.[113]

Bakha did not understand what the Colonel was saying, though he said, 'Han, Sahib, I know.' According to the novelist the Colonel was trying to make a distinction between himself and other ordinary sahibs in India. But for Bakha all the sahibs were sahibs. So the Colonel tried to make his position more clear.

> 'I am a padre and my God is Yessuh Masih (Jesus Christ)', emphasised the Colonel...

> 'Who is Yessuh Masih, really, Sahib?' Bakha asked, eager to allay his curiosity.[114]

The Colonel took Bakha to the church and sang a hymn to him, which made Bakha repeat the same question; but the Colonel did not answer him. Instead he told Bakha that Jesus died for all, both the rich and the poor and for Brahman and the Bhangi (Dalit). At this stage the conversation between Colonel Hutchinson and Bakha took a serious turn.

> 'Han, han, Sahib, I understand,' said Bakha eagerly, 'Yessuh Masih makes no difference between the Brahmin and myself.'
>
> 'Han, han, my boy, we are all alike in the eyes of Jesus,' the Colonel answered him. But he began garrulously: 'He is Our King. He is the Son of God. We are all sinners. He will intercede with God, His Father, on our behalf.'
>
> 'He is superior to us. We are all sinners. Why, why is any one above another? Why are all sinners?' Bakha began to reflect.
>
> 'Why are we all sinners, Sahib?' he queried.
>
> 'We were all born sinners,' replied the Colonel evasively, the puritan in him shying at an exposition of the doctrine of original sin which seemed called for.
>
> 'We must confess our sins. Then alone will He forgive us, otherwise we will have to suffer the eternal torment of hell. You confess your sins to me before I convert you to Christianity.'
>
> 'But, Huzoor, I don't know who Yessuh Masih is. I know Ram. But I don't know Yessuh Masih'.
>
> 'Ram is the god of the idolators,' the Colonel said after a pause, and a bit absent-mindedly. 'Come and confess your sin to me and Yessuh Masih will receive you in Heaven when you die.'... 'Yessuh Masih must be a good man,' he (Bakha) thought, 'if he regards a Brahman and a Bhangi the same.' But who was he? Where did he come from? What did he do? He had heard the story of Ram. He had heard the story of Krishna. He hadn't heard story of Yessuh Masih. 'This Sahib will not tell me the story,' he said to himself. But he still hoped he might give him

> a pair of his cast-off trousers. And he followed him half unwillingly.[115]

While the conversation between the Sahib and Bakha was going on Sahib's wife Mary Hutchinson started calling him for tea. When the Sahib was getting late and was still talking with Bakha –

> So that the tea should get cold!' exclaimed Mary Hutchinson.
> I can't keep waiting for you all day, while you go messing about with all those dirty bhangis (sweeper) and chamars (a leather worker Dalit).' And saying this she withdrew into the house.[116]

Bakha did not understand what the Sahib's wife said. But after hearing the phrase "bhangis and chamars" he got the idea that something was wrong and for that he was responsible. So he got up to leave after saying 'Salaam (good day), Sahib.' The Sahib tried to stop him, but he left by taking a thought and saying to himself:

> Everyone thinks of us at fault'… 'He wants me to come and confess my sins. And his mem-sahib! I don't know what she said about bhangis and chamars. She was angry with the sahib I am sure I am the cause of the memsahib's anger. I didn't ask padre to come and talk to me. He came of his own accord. I was so happy talking to him. I would certainly have asked him for a pair of white trousers, had the memsahib not been angry.'[117]

Concluding Remarks

On the basis of the discussion in this chapter the following main points may be summed up:

First, the problem of the Christian Dalits is a living existing reality and has a direct relationship with the overall approach of the work and methodology of the missionaries which was later on carried on by the national Christian leaders in India.

Second, the religious concepts such as individual salvation, personal holiness and emphasis on other-worldliness became a means of escapism for the poor Dalits from the actual reality of their suffering and oppression instead of facing and fighting these evils.

Third, the overall Christian missionary and later Indian Christian approaches based upon their understanding of Christian religion, instead of leading Christian Dalits toward gaining their equal human dignity or basic rights, led them further into the captivity of the same problem.

NOTES AND REFERENCES

1. Letter of Paul to the Galatians (NRSV), 3:28.
2. Quoted in editorial: *The Examiner* (The Catholic News Review), 143/3. January 18.
3. *Ibid.*
4. Azariah, M: *The Un-Christian Side of the Indian Church (the plight of the Untouchable Converts),* Bangalore, 1986, p. 10
5. (a) Ambedkar, Dr. Babasaheb: "The Condition of the Convert," in *Dr. Babasaheb Ambedkar—Writings and Speeches* Vol. 5. Compiled by
   (b) Vasant Moon, The Education Department, Government of Maharashtra, Bombay, 1989, pp. 443-76.
6. Chaudhuri, Nirad C.: *The Continent of Circe (An Essay on the Peoples of India),* Bombay, 1983 (reprinted), p. 310.
7. *Ibid.*
8. Quoted by Fr. Shouri O.F.M. in "Dalit Christian in India", *The Examiner*, August 10, 1991, p. 11.
9. (a) *Report of the Backward Classes Commission* (popularly known as Mandal Commission), First Part, Volumes I & II, Government of India, New Delhi, 1980, p. 55.
   See for detailed discussion:
   (b) Fuller, C.J.: *Kerala Christians and the Caste System in Social Stratification,* Delhi, 1993 (second impression), pp. 195-212.
10. Thomas, M.M.: 'Foreword' to *An Introduction to Indian Christian Theology,* by Robin Boyd, Delhi, 1991 (reprinted), p. 'a' (prelims).
11. Examples:
    (a) "Christian Dalits and Caste in Churches", *Religion and Society,* Vol. XXXIV, No. 3, September 1987.
    (b) "Dalit Ideology", *Religion and Society,* Vol. XXXVI, No. 3, September 1990.

(c) "Dalit Theology", *Journal of Dharma*, Vol. XVI, No. 1, January–March 1991.
(d) Prabhakar, M.E. (ed.): *Towards a Dalit Theology*, Delhi, 1988.
(e) Irudayaraj, Xavier (ed.): *Emerging Dalit Theology*, Madurai, 1990.
(f) Nirmal, Arvind P. : *Towards a Common Dalit Ideology*, Madras, n.d.

12. Webster, John C.B.: *The Dalit Christians: A History*, ISPCK, Delhi, 1992.
13. In the first chapter of this book, Webster says: "the purpose of this chapter is to establish a nineteenth century starting point from which the subsequent history of dalit Christians can be traced." *Ibid.*, p. 7.
14. See Chapter One of this work.
15. Firth, Cyril Bruce: *An Introduction to Indian Church History*, Madras, 1981, p. 2ff.
16. Mathew, C.P. & M.M. Thomas: *The Indian Churches of Saint Thomas*, Delhi, 1967, p. 19.
17. Ibid, p. 20.
18. Kaye, John William: *Christianity in India: An Historical Narrative*, London, 1859, p. 15.
19. *Ibid.*, p. 16.
20. *Ibid*, p. 15.
21. *Ibid.*, p. 30.
22. *Ibid.*
23. Mandelbaum, David G.: *Society in India*, Bombay, 1990 (reprinted), p. 267.
24. (a) Irudayaraj, Xavier: *op. cit.*, p. 20.
    Also see:
    (b) Dumont, Louis: *Homo Hierarchicus, The Indian Caste System and its Implications*, Chicago, 1990, p. 204.
25. Kaye John William: *op. cit.*, p. 34.
26. *Ibid.*, p. 32.
27. *Ibid.*, p. 33.
28. *Ibid.*, pp. 65-74.
29. Heick, Otto W.: *A History of Christian Thought*, Volume II, Philadelphia, 1966, p. 23.
30. Weborg, John: "Pietism: The Fire of God which Flames in the Heart of Germany" in Frank C. Senn, (ed.), *Protestant Spiritual Traditions*, New York, 1986, pp. 199-202.
31. Kaye, John William: *op. cit.*, p. 71.
32. *Ibid.*, p. 81.
33. Andrews, Rev. C.F.: *North India*, Oxford, 1908, p. 1.
34. Kaye John William: *op. cit.*, p. 87.
35. Andrews, Rev. C.F.: *op. cit.*, p. 3.
36. *Ibid.*, pp. 3, 4.
37. Paul, Rajaiah D.: *The Cross over India*, London, p. 44.
38. Andrews, Rev. C.F.: *op. cit.*, p. 5.

39. Walker, F. Deaville: *William Carey, Missionary Pioneer and Statesman,* London, 1926, pp. 81, 87, 88.
40. Grant, John Webster: *God's People in India,* Madras, 1965 (reprint), p. 50.
41. Paul, Rajaiah D.: *op. cit.*, p. 54.
42. Smith, George: *The Life of Alexander Duff,* London, 1881, p. 108.
43. *Ibid.,* p. 115.
44. Andrew, Rev. C.F.: *op. cit.,* p. 24.
45. Smith, George: *op. cit.*, p. 113.
46. *Ibid.,* p. 51.
47. Kaye, John William: *op. cit.*, p. 289.
48. Andrew, Rev. C.F.: *op. cit.,* pp. 14, 15.
49. *Ibid.,* p. 20.
50. Kaye, John William: *op. cit.,* pp. 352, 353.
51. *Ibid.,* pp. 355, 356.
52. Newton, John: *Historical Sketches of the India Missions of the Presbyterian Church in the United States of America,* Allahabad, 1886, p. 1 (Preface).
53. Anderson, William B. and Charles R. Watson: *Far North in India,* Philadelphia, 1909, p. 184.
54. Webster, John C.B.. *The Christian Community and Change in the Nineteenth Century in North India,* Delhi, 1976. p. 47.
55. *Survey of the Evangelistic work of the Panjab Mission of the Presbyterian Church in the U.S.A.,* 1929, p. 25.
56. (a) Gordon, The Rev. Andrew: *Our India Mission, 1855-1885,* Philadelphia, 1888, pp. 421-8.
    Also see:
    (b) Stock, Frederick and Margert: *People Movements in the Panjab with Special Reference to the United Presbyterian Church,* Bombay, 1978 (reprint), pp. 64-7.
57. Gordon, The Rev. Andrew: *op. cit.,* p. 422.
58. *Ibid.*
59. Picket, J. Waskom: *Christian Mass Movement,* New York, 1933, p. 23.
60. Gordon, The Rev. Andrew: *op. cit.*, p. 424.
61. Pickett, J. Waskom: *op. cit.*, p. 45.
62. Vide, *ibid.,* pp. 51, 52.
63. Vide, *ibid.,* pp. 47-9.
64. Kaye, John William: *op. cit.,* p. 41.
65. Gordon, The Rev. Andrew: *op. cit.*, p. 446.
66. Clark, The Rev. Robert: *A Brief Account of Thirty Years of Missionary work of the Church Missionary Society in Panjab and Sindh, 1852-1882,* Lahore, 1883, p. 20.
67. Taylor, H.F. Lechmene: *In the Land of the Five Rivers, A sketch of the work of the Church of Scotland in the Panjab,* London, 1906, p. 85.
68. a) Webster, John C.B.: *op. cit.,* p. 34.
    b) Dharmaraj, Jacob S.: *Colonialism and Christian Mission: Postcolonial*

Reflections, Delhi, 1993, p. 138.

69. Newbigin, Leslie: *The Other Side of 1984*, Geneva, 1984, p. 1.
70. Andrews, Rev. C.F.: *op. cit.*, p. 161.
71. *Ibid.,* p. 164.
72. Chaudhuri, Nirad C.. *op. cit.*, p. 332.
73. Forrester, Duncan B.: *Caste and Christianity*, London, 1980, p. 70.
74. Tyndale Biscoe (of Kashmir): *An Autobiography,* London, 1946, p. 110.
75. *Ibid.,* p. 113.
76. Snell, Rev. C.D.: "Christianity in India" in *The Church Missionary Review*, LXVI/790, February 1915, p. 85.
77. The author of this present work has lived in Jullundher city (Panjab) from 1969-1974 and has seen such properties belonging to the converts from upper caste.
78. Again such an example can be seen today, if one visits Mission compounds in a city like Jullundher and Ludhiana in Panjab, one can meet such converts from lower caste living in small houses, who have worked for Missionaries as servants.
79. Juergensmeyer, Mark: *Religion as Social Vision, The Movement against Untouchability in 20th century Panjab*, Berkeley, 1982, p. 187.
80. *Ibid.,* p. 186.
81. J.C.R. Ewing's letter to Dr. Gillespie, March 19, 1894, cited in John C.B. Webster: *op. cit.*, p. 60.
82. (a) Cf. Juergensmeyer, Mark: *op. cit.*, p. 188.
    Also see:
    (b) Kaye, John William: *op. cit.*, p. 353.
    (c) Oddie, G.A.: *Social Protest in India*, New Delhi, 1978, p. 45.
83. Newton, John: *op. cit.,* p. 58.
84. Webster, John C.B.: *op. cit.*, 1992, p. 75.
85. Aixala, J.: *Jesuit Formation and Inculturation in India Today,* Anand, 1978, p. 23.
86. *Vide* (for details) Kananaikil, Jose: *Scheduled Castes in the Constituent Assembly*, New Delhi, 1982, p. 14.
87. Shastri, Shankaranand: *My Memories and Experiences of Babasaheb Dr. B.R. Ambedkar & His Contribution to the Nation,* Ghaziabad, 1989, pp. 33, 34
88. *Vide* (for the text of) the Constitution (Scheduled castes) Order, 1950 with amendment in *Constitutional Provisions for the Scheduled Castes,* by Jose Kananaikil, New Delhi, 1974, p. 39.
89. Bhattacharyya, N.N.: *Ancient Indian History and Civilization, Trends and Perspectives,* New Delhi, 1988, p. 157.
90. Kaye, John William: *op. cit.,* p. 353.
91. Chaudhuri, Nirad C.: *op. cit.,* p. 304.
92. *Ibid.,* p. 310.
93. *Ibid.,* p. 330.

94. *Ibid.*, p. 331.
95. *Ibid.*, p. 332.
96. *Ibid.*, p. 335.
97. *Ibid.*, p. 353.
98. Ambedkar, Dr. Babasaheb: *op. cit.*, p. 456ff.
99. *Ibid.*, p. 460ff.
100. *Ibid.*, p. 439.
101. *Ibid.*, pp. 439, 440.
102. *Ibid.*, p. 552.
103. Aixala, J.: *op. cit.*, p. 23.
104. Ambedkar, Dr. Babasaheb: *op. cit.*, p. 453.
105. *Ibid.*, p. 454.
106. *Ibid.*, pp. 473-4.
107. Anand, Mulk Raj: *Untouchable,* Bangalore, first published 1935 (revised 1981), p. 20.
108. *Ibid.*, p. 89.
109. *Ibid.*, p. 92.
110. *Ibid.*, p. 93.
111. *Ibid.*, p. 173.
112. *Ibid.*, pp. 167, 168.
113. *Ibid.*, pp. 138, 139.
114. *Ibid.*, p. 140.
115. *Ibid.*, pp. 144-6.
116. *Ibid.*, p. 147.
117. *Ibid.*, p. 148.

PART II

DALIT IDENTITY AND BASIC RIGHTS

CHAPTER THREE

Dalit Identity

Introduction

It was observed in Chapter One that almost all the historical sources mentioned had painted the image/identity of Dalits negatively. They had beaen treated merely as "object" instead of as "subject" In embracing religions other than Hinduism, their main motive or hope was to regain their lost identity or social status.[1]

To clarify this point further, in this chapter, two aspects of Dalit identity are discussed further: *first*, Dalit as object of history and *second*, Dalit as subject of history. The first aspect has been dealt with at length in Chapter One, and hence discussion on it will be brief. Discussion on the second aspect as "subject" will be offered more from the sources written by the Dalits themselves.

Dalits as Object of History

History

In general, authors of Indian history have treated the Dalits as "object". The "subject" of their historical writings always have been the opponents of the Dalits. For example Suniti Kumar Chatterji in his work *Indo-Aryan and Hindi*, has recognised the existence of pre-Aryan people of India as *Dasa, Dasyu* and *Nisadas,* whom he has also termed "the Original Indian Austic People" or "Aborigines" or "Dravidian".[2] But still they are not the subject of his work. The general term he has used for them is "non-Aryan", which shows that "Aryan" are his the subject, the others being just "non" One may note the following statement:

> It is now becoming more and more clear that the non-Aryan contributed by far the greater position in the fabric of Indian civilization, and a great deal of Indian religious and cultural traditions, of ancient legend and history, is just non-Aryan translated in terms of the Aryan speech.[3]

One needs to note the phrases "non-Aryan" or "Indian civilization", in the above quotation. "Non-Aryan" of course are conquered *Dasas,* who according to Suniti Kumar Chatterji, later on were divided into two groups, Sudras (the serving caste) and the slaves (present Dalits), and the Arya according to him are Vaisya, Ksatriya and Brahman.[4] But the interesting thing is the *Dasa* groups, whom he himself has accepted as "original Indian". If that is true, then "Indian civilisation" should have been theirs; and newcomers who settled after conquering "the original Indian" should have been treated as contributors to the ongoing "Indian civilisation". This is where the question of "subject" or "object" of Indian history arises.

Of course in one sense all these written histories are representative of some set of "ideological interests". This is the main thesis which Romila Thapar has developed in the first chapter of her work *Interpreting Early India.* She has stated her thesis in these words:

> In Europe, post-Renaissance interests, which initiated the extensive study of the ancient study, brought to this study the ideological concerns of their own time. These concerns are also reflected in the Historiography of India, if not of Asia. The interpretation of Indian history from the eighteenth century onwards relates closely to the world view of Europeans, and particularly British historians, who provided the initial historiographical base. The resulting theories frequently reflected, whether consciously or not, the political and ideological interests of Europe, the history of India becoming one of the means of propagating those interests.[5]

Thapar cites a number of examples of Europeans, particularly from British background, whose ideology-based Indian historiography suited the cause of colonial rule. The most powerful and influential theory was of the Aryans. According to it most of the Aryans were a branch of Indo-European race and language groups, who invaded North India around 1500 B.C., conquered the indigenous peoples and "established the Vedic Aryan culture which became the foundation of Indian culture".[6] Thapar also says that this race theory "has not only served cultural nationalism in India, but continues to serve Hindu revivalism and, inversely, anti-Brahmin movements".[7] She also referred to the nationalist historical writing which, according to her has laid more importance on religion in Indian society. The nationalist historians were concerned only with those ideas which were related to the national problem. In a nutshell what one sees in her discussion is the role of "ideology" in writing the historical interpretation.

Romila Thapar's thesis is equally applicable to all the writings from the Rigvedic times onwards till now. All of them have treated the Dalits as "object". Reflecting this truth, Thapar herself has given a number of examples from the *Rigveda, Mahabharata* and *Puranas* to prove that a number of historical myths were created to legitimise some of the prevailing aspects of the social or religious life of that time. For example, the *Purusa sukta* hymn of the *Rigveda* has provided a myth, which not only describes the origin of the four castes, but also provides a system of social sanction particularly through caste to deny the *Sudhra varna* the right of establishing lineage "since it is said more often to include groups identified by the status of the two parents".[8] The myth of *Prithu* was created "to legitimise the expulsion of such groups when land was cleared and settled by agriculturists". According to the story a King Vena became wicked for not performing the sacrificial ritual and had to be killed by the *risis,* who alone had the right to depose rulers. The *risis* churned Vena's left thigh for his successor and *Nisada* came out, who was inadequate, a dark, short and ugly man; therefore *Nisada* was expelled to the forest as a hunter. From him started all the communities of forest-dwelling people. *Risis* then from the right arm of Vena churned King Prithu, who was a cattle-keeping agriculturist.[9]

In the *Itihasa-purans* tradition, Thapar sees the basis of "historical consciousness", which, according to her "has often been assumed, takes the form of historical writing".[10] If this is true, then the first task before the Dalit historian or those historians who have concern for them is to demythologise those ancient myths and stories which continue to be used till date to keep Dalits at the level of object.

Now it looks as though a number of both non-Dalit and Dalit scholars have become conscious of "Dalit being treated as object of history". Some of them are being referred to in the next section.

Dalits as "Subject" of History

In the past, literature about the Dalits or written by them has included some study-based publications, which Association Press (YMCA) brought out between 1920 and 1940. In these studies an attempt was made not only to present the views of the Dalits, but also to bring out some positive elements of their past lost identity and heritage. For example, Briggs in his work on *The Chamars* says that he interviewed people living in villages and towns, who are working as farmers, tanners, shoemakers, wizards, gurus and servants and his "single aim has been in all cases to record the *Chamars'* point of view".[11] Alexander Robertson's study on *The Mahar Folk* appeared in 1938. In the foreword to this work John McKenzie, the former principal of Wilson College, Bombay, says that Robertson "presents to us (the Chamar) not as a mere object of scientific interest, but as a man, and as a man possessing all the worth and dignity, and all the capacity for practical, intellectual and spiritual attainment, that are found in other members of God's great family."[12] Space does not allow more examples from these works, to show they have tried to present the life of the Dalits from *their* point of view.

Notable among the more recent studies, which are also of a more scientific nature, is *Untouchable: An Indian Life History* by James Freeman,[13] in which the writer presents details of an Orissa Dalit named Muli of 40 mostly in Muli's own words, which looks like an autobiography. The main question which this work addresses is, what happens when an untouchable attempts to break out of his accepted role? Worthy of mention is also a study of the movement against untouchability in the twentieth century

Panjab, entitled *Religion as Social Vision*,[14] This work, which analyses cases of Chamars and Churas of the Panjab deals mainly with the question: "What happens when untouchables decide that they are not Hindus to subscribe to the concepts undergirding castes, concepts many untouchables regard as oppression?"

An early example of the novel as a literary form for presenting the Dalit perspective was Mulk Raj Anand's *Untouchable*, through its protagonists Bakha and his father Lakha. On one occasion, when Lakha tries to make Bakha understand the reality of their life, Bakha answers: "But they think we are mere dirt, because we clean their dirt."[15] According to the novelist, Lakha understands the real reason why the upper castes treat them as "dirt". He tells Bakha, "We must realise that it is religion which prevents them from touching us." But the novelist adds, "He (Lakha) never throughout his narrative renounces his deep-rooted sense of inferiority and the docile acceptance of the laws of fate."[16]

Among the writings in which the authors have tried to present the cause of the Dalits, from their own perspective[17] the most noteworthy is *Beyond The Four Varnas* by Prabhati Mukherjee,[18] which throws a good deal of light on the historical roots of the Dalits. A good record of the firsthand views of the Dalits themselves is found in Barbara R. Joshi's *Untouchable! Voice of the Dalit Liberation Movement.*[19] Lata Murugkar's *Dalit Panther Movement in Maharashtra* presents a sociological appraisal of the Dalit movement or problem from the point of view of Dalits.[20] Eleanor Zelliot's *From Untouchable to Dalit* highlights Ambedkar's role in the Dalit movement, which the author calls "Ambedkar Movement" [21]

Writings by Dalits themselves treating Dalits as the "subject" of history are of two kinds. The first includes: poetry, autobiographies, short stories, essays and speeches. The lead in this category has been given by Marathi Dalit writers. Two anthologies of their work translated into English recently are: *Poisoned Bread* edited by Arjun Dangle[22] and *An Anthology of Dalit Literature* edited by Mulk Raj Anand and Eleanor Zelliot.[23] These collections of Marathi Dalits, beside revealing the deep inner agony in the very humanness of the Dalits, also tell the readers that the Dalits have now broken their centuries-old silence imposed upon them by the caste-structured society. The following few verses from these anthologies reveal the changing status of the Dalits in human history, from object to subject. Arjun Dangle in his poem "Revolution", says:

> We used to be their friends
> when, clay pots hung from our necks,
> brooms tied to our rumps,
> We made our rounds through the upper lane
> calling "Ma-bap, Johar, Ma-bap"...
> Today we see a root-to-crown change.
> Crows-jackals-dog-vulture-kites
> are our closest friends
> The upper lane doors are closed to us.
> "Shout Victory to the Revolution"
> "Shout Victory"
> "Burn, burn those who strike at tradition."[24]

The editor's note under the poem says that the call to "Shout Victory to the Revolution" "is a quotation from a Brahman poet. Dangle's point is that while the elite call for revolution, those who revolt are burnt." It is true now the Dalits also have recognised themselves as full human beings, which means a "subject" of their history. This truth we find in the following verses of Sharan Kumar Limlale's poem "White paper":

> I do not ask
> for the sun and moon from your sky
> your farm, your land,
> your high houses or your mansions
> I do not ask for gods or rituals,
> castes or sects
> or even for your mother, sister, daughters
> I ask for
> my rights as a man...
> My rights: contagious caste riots
> festering city by city, village by village,
> man by man

For that's what my rights are –
Sealed off, outcast, road-blocked, exiled
I want my rights, give my rights.
Will you deny this incendiary state of things?
uproot the scriptures like railway tracks,
Burn like a city bus your lawless laws
My friends
My rights are rising like the sun
Will you deny this sunrise?[25]

The second kind of a few written works have tried to go to the historical roots of the Dalits. In this direction a beginning was made by B.R. Ambedkar in his various speeches and writings, during the 1930s and 1940s. But his major work in this direction was published in 1948 with the title Th*e Untouchables,* in which he dealt specially with two questions: "Who were they? And why did they become untouchables?" Ambedkar has even hinted at the common roots of three groups of people, namely 1) the Criminal Tribes, 2) the Aboriginal Tribes (Tribals), and 3) the Untouchables (Dalits). He has made Hindu civilisation responsible for bringing these three sections of society to their present state. He says about it:

> What else can be said of a civilisation which has produced *a mass of people* who are taught to accept crime as an approved means of earning their livelihood, *another mass of people* who are left to live in full bloom of their primitive, barbarism in the midst of civilization and *a third mass of people* who are treated as an entity beyond human intercourse and whose mere touch is enough to cause pollution?[26]

Ambedkar asserted that the Dalits are equal to Hindus racially. He called them "Broken men".[27] Here again the truth of the Dalits being human beings is recognised, which they "were" and "are" and they have to achieve.

Among the other Dalit writers who have recognised the lost human identity of Dalits is O.P. Das, born of a Dhobi (washerman) family of West Bengal, who in his work *The Untouchable Story* referred to Dalits as "faceless" people. He says, "The Indian Untouchables form a thick crust of faceless and nameless human anthill which have no singer of their own agonies. In the social arena, it is high caste Hindu reformers who weep for them."[28]

Concluding Remarks

The basic issue for the Dalits in India is to regain the fuller human self-identity (or get their face back), which also means to become the subject of their own history. From the discussion in this chapter and also the earlier discussions it is clear that the main motive or purpose behind the various efforts made including the change of religion from Hinduism to others (such as Buddhism, Islam, Christianity, Sikhism) by the Dalits has been to gain their lost identity or to establish a new identity. The identity issue as seen in the examples from Dalit literature also includes the recovery of their basic human rights.

NOTES AND REFERENCES

1 See for detail discussion in this point:
a) Gokhale, Jayashree: *From Concessions to Confrontation*, Bombay, 1993, pp. 156-8.
b) Mandelbaum, David G.: *Society in India*, Bombay, 1990 (reprinted), pp. 523-5.
c) Gore, M.S.: *The Social Context of Ideology, Ambedkar's Political and Social Thought*, New Delhi, 1993, pp. 51, 52.
2. Chatterji, Suniti Kumar: *Indo-Aryan and Hindi*, Calcutta, 1969, pp. 18, 36. 47.
3. *Ibid.*, p. 33.
4. *Ibid.*, p. 50.
5. Thapar, Romila: *Interpreting Early India*, Oxford, 1992, pp. 1, 2.
6. *Ibid.*, p. 3.
7. *Ibid.*, p. 18.
8. *Ibid.*, p. 141.

9. *Ibid.*, p. 142.
10. *Ibid.*, p. 137.
11. Briggs, Geo. W.: *The Chamars*, Calcutta, 1920, p. 38.
12. Robertson, Alexander: *The Mahar Folk*, Calcutta, 1938, p. xii (foreword).
13. Freeman, James M.: *Untouchable—An Indian Life History*, London, 1979.
14. Juergensmeyer, Mark: *Religion as Social Vision (The Movement against Untouchability in 20th Century Panjab)*, Berkeley, 1982.
15. Anand, Mulk Raj: *Untouchable*, Bangalore, 1935 (revised 1981), p. 89.
16. *Ibid.*, p.93.
17. Examples:
    a) Srivastava, Suresh Narain: *Harijans in Indian Society*, Aminabad, 1980.
    b) Sharma S.: *Sudra in Ancient India*, Delhi, 1990 (3rd rev. edn.).
18. Mukherjee, Prabhati: *Beyond the Four Varnas, The Untouchables in India*, Delhi, 1988.
19. Joshi, Barbara R. (ed.): *Untouchable! Voice of the Dalits Liberation Movement*, New Delhi, 1986.
20. Murugkar, Lata: *Dalit Panther Movement in Maharashtra*, Bombay, 1991.
21. Zelliot, Eleanor: *From Untouchable to Dalit*, New Delhi, 1992.
22. Dangle, Arjun (ed.): *Poisoned Bread* (Translations from Modern Marathi Dalit Literature), Bombay, 1992.
23. Anand, Mulk Raj and Eleanor Zelliot (eds.): *An Anthology of Dalit Literature* (poems), New Delhi, 1992.
24. *Ibid.*, pp. 43-4.
25. Dangle, Arjun (ed.): *op.cit.*, pp. 64-5.
26. Ambedkar, B.R.: 'The Untouchables' *in Dr. Babasaheb Ambedkar's Writings and Speeches*, edited by Vasant Moon, Vol. 7, Education Department, Government of Maharashtra, 1991, p. 239.
    Also see for Jotirao Phule's view on the same issue:
    O'Hanlon, Rosalind: *Caste, Conflict & Ideology*, Bombay, 1985, pp. 131-2.
27. *Ibid.*, p. 242.
28. Das, D.P.: *The Untouchable Story*, New Delhi, 1985, p. x (introduction).

CHAPTER FOUR

Christian Dalits and Basic Rights

Introduction

As has been pointed out in Chapters One and Three, the Dalits' severest loss is the loss of their human identity. The basic task before them is to recover their human dignity which they have lost because of the centuries-old oppression which they have faced. This is the common issue which the Dalits belonging to all faiths have to face together. But as was pointed out in Chapter Two, the case of Christian Dalits still becomes special, because they have been denied their basic human rights, including constitutional fundamental rights, which the Dalits professing Hinduism, Sikhism and Buddhism are enjoying. It has also been discussed in Chapter Two how the problems of Christians are similar; in general, this has been also recognised by the major Christian traditions and churches in India. A number of individuals and Government-appointed commissions have also accepted the position of the Christian Dalits.

It has been pointed out in Chapter Two how the Christian Dalits are suffering from threefold discrimination, (a) along with all the Dalits in general, (b) on the basis of "religion" at the hands of their own Government, and, (c) from their fellow Christians belonging to the upper castes/classes. This threefold discrimination makes the Christian Dalits' case special, which needs further investi-gation. As part of the investigation it is necessary to study the background of certain constitutional or administrative terms and how these are defined, which includes the expression "Scheduled Castes", which the Government of India has used for Dalits. Secondly, detailed reference is needed at least to one of the

Government-appointed commissions (that is Mandal Commision), which tried to deal with the problem of Christian Dalits. Finally, this investigation will refer to some remedies which the Government of India has provided for the protection of Dalits, yet how, because these are not applicable to the Christian Dalits, they lose their basic human rights and fundamental rights. These include Protection of Civil Rights Act, 1955; Protection of Civil Rights Rules, 1979, and Scheduled Castes and Scheduled Tribes (Prevention of Atrocities) Act, 1989. For convenience sake this investigation is being done under three subheads:

I. The Scheduled Castes and the 1950 Presidential Order;
II. Mandal Commission and Christians of Scheduled Caste Origin; and
III. Basic Rights of Christian Dalits and Governmental legislation.

The Scheduled Castes and the 1950 Presidential Order

Under this section, we need to consider the ambit of the expression "Scheduled Castes" and the criteria used for deciding its denotation.

The Expression "Scheduled Castes"

The expression "Scheduled Castes" was first coined by the Simon Commission (appointed by the British Government) between 1929 and 1932 and was later incorporated in the Government of India Act of 1935.[1] Prior to this, "Depressed classes" was used in Government (British) circles, and also by members of various reform movements.[2] The expression was used more or less for all kinds of depressed people including the "Untouchables", without differentiating on the basis of religion. It was in 1932 that for the first time the expression "Depressed Classes" was used exclusively for the Untouchables. The British Government was then trying to help all other communities such as Muslims, Christians, Anglo-Indians, and others (who, according to them, did not come under the Depressed Classes) and extending to them special benefits including giving them separate communal electorates.[3]

In 1931 a special committee was set up to draw a 'Schedule' of the castes covered under the Depressed Classes. The same year the Round Table Conference in London was convened in which from the Indian side Gandhi and Ambedkar were the key members. Here Ambedkar demanded separate electorate for the Depressed Classes, whom he always referred to as the Untouchables. But Gandhi objected. Ambedkar also suggested that Untouchables should be renamed "Protestant Hindu" or "Non-conformist Hindu".[4] By that time, of course, Gandhi had also introduced another term for Untouchables, that is, "Harijan" (meaning children of God), which he took from a Gujarati poem. But, this was not accepted or liked by the Untouchables themselves.[5] As Gandhi and Ambedkar did not agree (at the Round Table Conference), no final decision was taken. Finally the matter of communal electorates was left to the chairman of the Conference, Prime Minister Ramsay Macdonald, who in 1932 issued the Communal Award in which he also replaced the expression "the Depressed Classes" with "the Scheduled Castes".[6] From then onwards the Untouchables of India were known as the Scheduled Castes. Later the expression the Scheduled Castes was included in the Government of India Act, 1935, which was followed by the Government of India (Scheduled Castes) Order, 1936, according to which "no Indian Christian ... should be deemed a member of a Scheduled Caste".[7] This was the first time that "religion" was used as a criterion to define Scheduled Castes. (At this stage the effect of this decision was not felt by Indian Christians, as they were still enjoying the status of a minority community.) The complete definition of the expression the Scheduled Castes was also given in the Government of India Act, 1935, which said:

> "The Scheduled Castes" means such castes, races or tribes or parts or groups within castes, races, tribes, parts or groups which appear to the Governor—generally to correspond to the classes of persons formerly known as the Depressed Classes as the Governor-General may by order specify.[8]

This definition of the Scheduled Castes, more or less literally, was adopted by the authors of the Indian Constitution and later by the Government of India in 1950. The Indian Constitution's exact words are given in Article 366, clause 24:

> "Scheduled Castes" means such castes, races or tribes or parts of or groups within such castes, races or tribes as are deemed under Article 341 to be Scheduled Castes for the purpose of this Constitution.[9]

Marc Galanter has summed up the history of the expression "Scheduled Castes" in these words:

> "Scheduled Castes" is the most recent of a long line of official euphemisms for "Untouchables". The Scheduled Caste category is intended to comprise of those groups isolated and disadvantaged by their "untouchability"—that is, their low status in the traditional Hindu caste hierarchy which exposed them to invidious treatment, severe disabilities, and deprivation of economic, social, cultural and political opportunities. In the early years of the century the "depressed classes" (as they were classed) became an important focus of concern among reformers. After 1901, fears of diminished Hindu majorities and proposals for special legislative representation for these classes propelled "Untouchability" from the realm of philanthropy into the political arena.[10]

Finally, to sum up early history of the expression "Scheduled Castes"—this expression was used for those who were kept outside the fourfold *varna* system, and were called *avarnas.* They were also called *Chandalas, Panchamas* and such other contemptuous terms. Now they are called the Untouchables. In legal parlance they are known as the "Scheduled Castes",[11] but, as mentioned earlier Dalits have taken a title or name for themselves, which not only describes them as people, but also denotes their real state of deprivation. This title is "Dalit".

Criterion

The Indian Constitution, on the basis of its Article 341(1) only empowers the President of India, "...by public notification, to specify the castes, races or tribes or parts of or groups within castes, races or tribes which shall, for the purpose of this Constitution be deemed to be Scheduled Castes..."[12] Again, the Constitution without defining who is of a Schedled Caste in Article 366(24) only refers to the power given to the President of India in Article 341.[13] But once the President has issued such an order saying who can be included in the list or Schedule, this list of Scheduled Castes, on the basis of Article 342(2) can be changed only through an Act of Parliament.

While exercising the powers conferred on him in Article 341(1), the President of India promulgated in 1950 an order known as The Constitution (Scheduled Castes) Order, 1950. This Order of 1950 almost has re-enacted the list of the Government of India (Scheduled Castes) Order, 1936.[14] As stated earlier, concerning the Scheduled Castes, the Indian Constitution has followed all the bases that the British Government had laid down in 1936. Reference has already been made to the list, but the fundamental criterion of the Government of India (Scheduled Castes) Order, 1936 has been used by the Order of 1950 also. On that basis, the third paragraph of this Order reads:

> Notwithstanding anything contained in paragraph 2, no person who professes a religion different from Hindu shall be deemed to be a member of a Scheduled Caste.

This paragraph was amended in 1956 by Parliament to read "the Hindu or the Sikh" and again in May 1990 to "the Hindu or the Sikh or the Buddhist".

The British Government did include various other tests also to decide the Scheduled Castes list. Stephen Fuchs says: "The test applied for inclusion in the list was the social, educational and economic backwardness arising out of historical customs of untouchability".[15] J.H. Hutton, the Census Commissioner in 1931, worked out the following nine tests to identify the Scheduled Castes:

1. Whether the caste or class in question can be served by clean Brahmans or not.
2. Whether the caste or class in question can be served by the barbers, water-carriers, tailors, etc., who serve the caste Hindus.
3. Whether the caste in question pollutes a high-caste Hindu by contact or by proximity.
4. Whether the caste or class in question is one from whose hands a caste Hindu can take water.
5. Whether the caste or class in question is debarred from using public conveniences, such as roads, ferries, wells or schools.
6. Whether the caste or class in question is debarred from the use of Hindu temples.
7. Whether in ordinary social intercourse a well-educated member of the caste or class in question will be treated as an equal by high-caste men of the same educational qualifications.
8. Whether the caste or class in question is merely depressed on account of its own ignorance, illiteracy, or poverty, and but for that, would be subject to no social disability.
9. Whether it is depressed on account of the occupation followed, and whether but for that occupation it would be subject to no social disability.[16]

Hutton's tests may not apply *in toto* in the case of the Scheduled Caste people but the general implications of these tests are still valid. Galanter has discussed in detail these tests in his work *Competing Equalities.*[17] Besides J.H. Hutton, G.S. Pal of the Indian Franchise Commission, 1932, had used three general tests: "Socially despised; then there is economic backwardness; and educational bankruptcy".[18]

The position of the President and Parliament is more or less the same as that of the British Government in 1935-36, but a political party like the Bharatiya Janata Party (BJP) has a still more orthodox and biased criterion for dealing with the question of the Scheduled Castes, as explained in Chapter One.

It is true that originally it was the British Government which in 1935-36, introduced "religion" as a criterion and debarred the Christians of Scheduled Caste origin from getting the concessions and facilities available to members of other religions of Scheduled Caste origin. The same basis was used to debar Christian Dalits from these facilities and concessions in 1950 when the Presidential Order was promulgated. Until 1947, Christians in general enjoyed minority rights. But then three Christians, who happened to be members of the Constituent Assembly, became satisfied with fundamental rights and because of their action in 1950, Christians in India forever lost their basic minority rights also. Now the Christian Dalits neither have full fundamental rights nor other rights, as a result of which they have to continue to suffer all the discrimination, in spite of the fact that a number of arguments have been put forward by different individuals and commissions.

Mandal Commission and the Dalit Christians

Besides the Mandal Commission a number of commissions appointed by different State Governments also have sympatheti-cally considered the case of the Christians. This is particularly true of the commissions appointed by the governments of Kerala, Tamil Nadu and Karnataka. Besides Christians themselves[19] tackling the myth regarding the Christian converts from Scheduled Castes – that after becoming Christian, they automatically improve their social and political status – the various State Commissions have also made constructive observations. For example the Karnataka Backward Classes Commission of 1952 observed that

> A Scheduled Caste (man) might have made some progress, or might have embraced Islam or Christianity, and thereby the disabilities under which he suffered as a result of untouchability, might have, to some extent, disappeared. But the fact remains that such castes, tribes and racial groups still continue to suffer under other social, educational and economic handicaps and taboos.[20]

Besides the various State Commissions before these, the first Backward Classes Commission headed by Kaka Kalelkar also observed the practice of untouchability among South Indian Christians, and the influence of caste among Indian Christians. But Mandal Commission Report has taken far more seriously the case of Christians. In its section on "Evidence by Central and State Governments", it has observed that "In Kerala, Muslim, Latin Catholic and Anglo-Indian and Scheduled Caste converts to Christianity form three of the eight groups for whom separate reservations have been made."[21]

In the section "Evidence by the Public" suggestions favouring the same benefits for Christians of Scheduled Caste origin are clearly made. The Mandal Commission Report while taking note of an important suggestion made by Madhu Dandavate, has summarised his views as follows:

> Prof. Madhu Dandavate stated that conversion from one faith to another did not change the socio-economic status of a person. It was, therefore, desirable that converts from Scheduled Castes to Buddhism, Christianity etc. should be treated as Scheduled Castes. But until this change was brought about by legislation, all such converts should be listed as OBCs.[22]

Mandal Commission Report has also given the summary of a number of other responses on the question of Christians along with others. It says:

> In view of this, Scheduled Caste converts to Christianity, Islam, Buddhism etc., should not be denied the benefit extended to Scheduled Castes and the same should hold good in respect of OBCs. At some places, it was also contended that all Muslims and all Christians should be included in the list of OBCs as these communities were really very backward.[23]

Mandal Commission Report without any doubt has concluded that among Indian Christians caste is a reality. According to it "social and educational backwardness among" the Christian community is more or less the same as among Hindu communities.

Though the caste system is peculiar to Hindu society, in actual practice, it also pervades Christians. Elaborating further, it says:

> There are two reasons for this phenomenon: first, caste system is a great conditioner of the mind and leaves an indelible mark on a person's social consciousness and cultural mores. Consequently, even after conversion, the ex-Hindus carried with them their deeply ingrained ideas of social hierarchy and stratification.... Secondly, non-Hindu minorities living in predominantly Hindu India could not escape from its dominant social and cultural influence. Thus, both from within and without, caste amongst non-Hindu communities received continuous sustenance and stimulus.[24]

The Mandal Commission Report has accepted the reality of castes among Indian Christians, as in any other community. To substantiate this view, it has taken the example of the Christian community in Kerala, which, according to the Mandal Commission Report, is not only divided into various denominations on the basis of beliefs and rituals, but also "into various ethnic groups on the basis of their caste background." The report continues:

> ...even after conversion, the lower caste converts were continued to be treated as Harijans by all sections of the society, including the Syrian Christians... It was found that the Syrian and the Pulaya members of the same Church conducted religious rituals separately in separate buildings... Thus lower caste converts to a very egalitarian religion like Christianity... even after generations were not able to efface their caste background.[25]

The Mandal Commission Report did not stop at making an analysis of the conditions of the Christians of Scheduled Caste origin. It also made an effort to identify the percentage of these Christians. The criteria that it used for this purpose were not the same as it used to identify the Backward Classes having a Hindu background. The Commission used the following two criteria to identify people belonging to Other Backward Classes among the non-Hindus, including Christians:

(i) All untouchables converted (to Christianity).
(ii) Such occupational communities which are known by the name of their traditional hereditary occupation and whose Hindu counterparts have been included in the list of Hindu OBCs.[26]

On the basis of these criteria, according to the Mandal Commission Report, percentage wise, there are 0 44 per cent Christians of Scheduled Caste origin, which on the basis of the 1981 Census will be around thirty lakhs. But it seems these figures are based on figures of those Christians who have revealed their background to the Commission. Otherwise this should be over one crore (more than 50 per cent of the total population of Christians, which in 1981 was 16,168,447, without the figures of Assam State). In Volume VI of the report, the list of Other Backward Classes from 21 states has been given. Out of 21 states only the following twelve states' lists include Christians of Scheduled caste origin:[27]

(1) Andhra Pradesh: Christian Dombs and Scheduled Caste converts to Christianity, and their children;
(2) Gujarat: Khristi Gujarati Christian (converts from Scheduled Castes only);
(3) Kerala: Christian Domb and Scheduled Castes converted to Christianity;
(4) Madhya Pradesh: Scheduled Castes converted to Christianity;
(5) Maharashtra: Christians converted from Scheduled Castes;
(6) Orissa: Christian Domb;
(7) Punjab: converted Christians from Scheduled Castes;
(8) Tamil Nadu: converts to Christianity from Scheduled Castes irrespective of the generation of conversion;
(9) West Bengal: Scheduled Castes converted to Christianity;
(10) Chandigarh: Scheduled Caste converts to Christianity;

(11) Goa, Daman & Diu: Christian Chamar and Christian Mahar; and
(12) Pondicherry: Converts to Christianity from Scheduled Castes.

In brief, the Mandal Commission Report has uncovered one fact that the Christians of Scheduled Caste origin (Christian Dalits) suffer the same disabilities as their counterparts belonging to other religions.

Basic Rights of Christian Dalits and Governmental Acts

Under the 1950 Presidential Order, the Christian Dalits do not enjoy equal rights with their counterparts belonging to other religions. These rights include: reservation of seats in the House of the People (Article 330), reservation of seats in the Legislative Assemblies of States (Article 332), claims to government services and posts (Article 335), special officer to look after their interests (Article 338) and promotion of educational and economic interests (Article 46).[28] Through the use of these rights the Dalits partly can progress, but all these rights are denied to the Christian Dalits and it is done on the basis of the Presidential Order, which as amended in 1990 is known as 'The Constitution (Scheduled Castes) Orders (Amendment) Act 1990'. The Act only gives the above rights to those Dalits who profess "the Hindu or the Sikh or the Buddhist" (religions).[29]

A Christian Dalit, by profession a cobbler, Soosai challenged the validity of the discriminatory Presidential Order 1950 on the basis of religion. His case went to the highest court of the country. While dismissing his writ petition on September 30, 1986, the Division Bench of the Supreme Court of India, consisting of the Chief Justice P.N. Bhagwati, Justice R.S. Pathak and Justice A.N. Sen made the following remarks:

> It is not sufficient to show that the same caste continues after conversion. It is necessary to establish further that the discriminatin and handicaps suffered from membership of such

> caste continue in their oppressive severity in the new environment of a different religious community.[30]

The case of the Christian Dalits was also debated during the summer session of Parliament (May 1990), when the last amendment was made to the Presidential Order of 1950. A number of members, both Christians and those belonging to other faiths, argued in favour of the Christian Dalits. During the discussion two main points were raised against the Christian Dalits. First, why Christian Dalits should not be given equal rights. In this regard, Uma Bharati argued:

> Point of Order. Dividing the Christians into *Harijan* Christian and high-caste Christians, I think the hon. member has to ask the permission of John Pope Paul. He does not divide Christians into *Harijan* Christians and *Savarna* Christians. According to the Christian religion there is no *Harijan* and no *Savarna,* all are equal. What the hon. member is saying is against the Christian religion (interruptions).[31]

As to why a Buddhist Dalit should be granted equal rights, Kalka Das said:

> Had he not understood the importance of Buddhism, its Indian identity and its inseparable links with Hinduism, he (Ambedkar) could have embraced Islam or Christianity, but he did not turn to any foreign religion.[32]

Finally at the end of May 1990 debate, Parliament once again could not extend equal rights to the Christian Dalits. What is the implication of this act of Parliament? First, it means that Christian Dalits continue to lose one of their most important fundamental rights, which prohibits any kind of discrimination on the basis of religion which has been stated in Article 15 of the Constitution in these words:

> The State shall not discriminate against any citizen on grounds only of religion, race, caste, sex, place of birth or any of them.[33]

Article 25 makes two points further clear:

> all persons are equally entitled to freedom of conscience and the right freely to profess, practise and propagate religion.[34]

Second, besides depriving the Christiasn Dalits of their fundamental rights concerning religion, the Presidential Order of 1950 has a much deeper implication. The Government of India has brought out a number of other Acts and Rules in order to give protection to the Dalits, which include Protection of Civil Rights Act, 1955; Protection of Civil Rights Rules, 1977; and Scheduled Castes and Scheduled Tribes (Prevention of Atrocities) Act, 1989. Protection of Civil Rights Act, 1955 deals with the question of religion and social disabilities met by the Dalits and how the offenders can be punished. Along with other matters it also deals with the punishment for other offences arising out of "Untouchability". In short, it is "an Act to prescribe punishment for the preaching and practice of 'Untouchability', for the enforcement of any disability arising therefrom and for matters connected therewith."[35] The Protection of Civil Rights Rules, 1977, has given power to any State Government to appoint an officer not below the rank of a subdivisional magistrate for the purpose of making an enquiry concerning the protection of any civil rights.[36] The 1989 Act for Prevention of Atrocities is "an Act to prevent the commission of offences of atrocities against members of the Scheduled Castes and the Scheduled Tribes, to provide for Special Courts for the trial of such offences and for the relief and rehabilitation of the victims of such offences and for matters connected therewith or incidental thereto."[37]

It is clear from the contents of above Acts that they have given some protection of rights to the Dalits, but it is also clear, both from the contents and their titles, that these are to provide protection only to those Dalits who are recognised either as Scheduled Castes or Scheduled Tribes. So again, what about the Christian Dalits? Are they protected under these Acts? The answer is 'no', because they are not recognised as the Schedules Castes (Dalits) like the Dalits belonging to other religions. What implication has it for the Christian Dalits? Here it may be worth referring to two actual incidents in one of the South Indian States, Andhra Pradesh, in 1985 and 1991 respectively, which may throw some light on the implications of these Protection Acts for the Christian Dalits.

The first incident took place on July 17, 1985 in a village named Karamchedu, Prakasam District. In this incident the Christian Dalits were attacked by the upper caste Hindus and the persons killed were Tella Yehoshua (Joshua), Tella Moshe (Moses), Muttiah (Matthew), Duddu Ramesh, Son of Yohan (John) and Duddu Abraham. The news was reported by a number of newspapers, All India Radio and Television, all these reporting that some Harijans (Dalits) had been killed by the upper castes. No report stated the fact that all of them were *Christian* Dalits. This killing was discussed in the Andhra Legislative Assembly, but again on the basis that all those killed were Harijans or members of the Scheduled Castes. A one-man Commission of Enquiry under Justice D.P. Desai was appointed by the Government of Andhra Pradesh to probe into the Karamchedu incident. The Commission enquired the case not on the basis of those killed being Christian Dalits, but only Madigas (a community belonging to a Scheduled Caste, which means by faith Hindu) and submitted its report on March 28, 1988.[38]

The incident of 1991 took place on August 6th, when a mob comprising upper caste Reddis and other non-Dalits raided a Dalit colony at Tsundura of Guntur District, where eight Dalits were killed. All those killed belonged to the Lutheran Christian tradition. According to a report "the carnage was sparked off by the anger of the Reddis against a Dalit young man (a graduate), who had been accused of stretching his legs forward and kicking a Reddi young man sitting in the front row in a cinema show, a month before (July 4th)..." This news was discussed at an all-India level including in Parliament. But again the basis of all discussions and enquiries was that some Dalits (not Christian Dalits) were killed.[39] The incident continued to appear in the national newspapers for many months.[40]

According to one analysis of Karanchedu incident of July 17, 1985, neither the Press including All India Radio nor even a High Court Judge could differentiate between the Harijans (Dalits in general) and the Harijan (Dalit) Christians for the purpose of reporting or enquiry.[41] But the important point which needs to be noted is that the victims of both incidents were Christian Dalits, who, according to the Presidential Order, 1950 are not considered to be Scheduled Castes, and are therefore not entitled to any protection and care, neither under the special Articles provided in the Constitution (numbers 330, 332, 335, 338 and 46), nor under the Scheduled Caste and the Scheduled Tribes (Prevention of Atrocities) Act, 1989 and Protection of Civil Rights Act, 1955. Here a question may even be raised if the Christian Dalits have a right to live, about which the United Nations Universal Declaration of Human Rights says in Article 3: "Everyone has the right to life, liberty and security of person."[42]

Concluding Remarks

From the discussion of this chapter on the basic rights of the Christian Dalits, the following three points become clear:

First, the Christian Dalits do not enjoy their full fundamental and protection rights given to their counterparts belonging to other religions under the Constitution of India.

Second, the Christian Dalits are denied the above rights because they are "Christian" by religion.

So finally *third,* the religious factor, it seems, becomes for the Christian Dalits more a source of problems or bondage than a source of liberation.

NOTES AND REFERENCES

1. See, Ouwerkerk, Louise: *The Untouchables of India,* London, 1945, pp. 40, 41.
2. See for details, Karnataka Backward Classes Commission, Government of Karnataka Report, Volume I, Part I, 1975, pp. 55-8.
3. Isaacs, Harold R.: *India's Ex-Untouchables,* Bombay, 1965, p. 36.
4. *Ibid.*
5. *Ibid.,* pp. 39-41.
6. Ouwerkerk, Louise: *op.cit.,* p. 41.
7. Galanter, Marc: *Competing Equalities—Law and the Backward Classes in*

India, Delhi, 1984, p. 143.

8. Cited in Karantaka Backward Classes Commissions Report, *op.cit.*, p. 60.
9. The Constitution of India (As modified upto August 15, 1989): Government of India, Ministry of Law and Justice, New Delhi, 1989, p. 205.
10. Galanter, Marc: *op. cit.*, p. 122.
11. Veeramani, K. and P.R. Kuppuswamy: *According to Law We Are still Shudras—But How*?, Madras, 1989, p. 2.
12. *The Constitution of India*, *op.cit.*, p. 203.
13. *Ibid.,* p. 205.
14. See Galanter, Marc: *op. cit.,* p. 132.
15. Fuchs, Stephen: *At the Bottom of Indian Society,* New Delhi, 1981, p. 2.
16. Hutton, J.H.: *Caste in India,* London, 1951, pp. 193-4.
17. Galanter, Marc: *op. cit.,* pp. 128-30.
18. *Ibid.,* p. 127.
19. See "Christian Dalits and Caste in Churches". *Religion and Society,* XXXIV/3, Bangalore, September 1987.
20. "Karnataka Backward Classes Commission (Constituted under the Commissions of Inquiry Act, 1952), Report," Volume I, Part I, Bangalore, 1975, p. 78.
21. "Report of the Backward Classes Commission", Government of India, First Part, Volumes I & II, 1980, pp. 38, 39.
22. *Ibid.,* p. 46.
23. *Ibid.,* p. 47.
24. *Ibid.,* p. 55.
25. *Ibid.,* p. 55.
26. *Ibid.,* p. 56.
27. Reservations for Backward Classes, Mandal Commission Report of the Backward Commission 1980, (Alongwith Introduction), Delhi, 1990, pp. 304, 309, 319, 322, 323, 329, 331, 335, 343, 346, 349, 352.
28. The Constitution of India, *op. cit.*, pp. 172-76 and p. 22.
29. The Scheduled Castes and Scheduled Tribes (Prevention of Atrocities Act, 1989 (No. 33 of 1989) and the Protection of Civil Rights Act 1955 (72 of 1955) with short notes, Lucknow, 1990, p. 1.
30. Rao, Kande Prasada: *Freedom of Religion for Harijan in India,* Ongole, 1990, p. 16.
31. Kananaikil, Jose: *Scheduled Caste Converts in Search of Justice, Constitution (Scheduled Castes), Orders (Amendment) Bill,* 1990, p. 5.
32. Ibid., p. 17.
33. *The Constitution of India*, op. cit., p. 7.
34. *Ibid.,* p. 17.
35. The Scheduled Castes and Scheduled Tribes (Prevention of Atrocities) Act 1989 and other (See note 29), *op. cit.,* p. 11.
36. *Ibid.,* p. 23.
37. *Ibid.,* p. 3.

38. See for details, Kande Prasada Rao: *op. cit.*, pp. 17-19.
39. See for details XVIII Biennial Council Meeting, Hyderabad, January 22-24, 1992, Christian Institute for the Study of Religion and Society and Joint Programmes, pp. 40-3.
40. *Indian Express*, Wednesday, December 2, 1992, Madras, p. 9.
41. Rao, Kande Prasada: *op. cit.*, p. 18.
42. Das, Bhagwan: *Human Rights and Constitutional Rights*, New Delhi, 1987, p. 2.

PART III

Dalits and Enabling Strategies

CHAPTER FIVE

Dalit Politics and the Christian Response

Introduction

In post-Independence India not much has been written on the subject of "Dalit politics",[1] except for a few chapters in books or articles.[2] So there is still a need for some comprehensive systematic work covering the post-Independence era. This chapter may be considered a small step in this direction. It is divided into the following sub-sections:

I. Dalits as a political force—a reality
II. Main factors responsible for the political awakening among the Dalits
III. Dalit politics after independence
  a) political parties
  b) dalits and the protests
  c) dalit solidarity programme
IV. Christians/Churches and the Dalit Issue
  a) Response of the Church
  b) Need for building political action.

Dalits as a Political Force—a Reality

On August 19, 1993, the *Times of India,* reported about a meeting of the Dalits and Indigenous political leaders belonging to the ruling Congress party. It is evidence about the existence of the reality of the Dalit movement as a political force. The report noted:

> The leaders of the backward castes (including Dalits) and tribes in the Congress (ruling party)... have raised their voice against the neglect of these sections of society and demanded firm measures to redress their grievances. They recently held a one-day meeting... It was demanded that the party should project a candidate from this section as the chief minister during the campaign for the assembly election. The idea was mooted by Mr. Ajit Jogi (a Christian Dalit), Rajya Sabha member... Almost all attributed the rise of the Bahujan Samaj Party (a Dalit political party) in certain regions of the state (Madhya Pradesh) to the discontent in this section...[3]

This report reveals the Dalit leaders' place in a major political party and also how the Dalit leaders belonging to the ruling party view the emergence of a Dalit-led political party. V.S. Naipaul, in *India—A Million Mutinies Now,* also reveals an insight into the dalit awakening, based upon his firsthand experience in Bombay. He writes:

> The Dalits, for instance. If they still have been only the mahatma's Harijans, children of God, people for whom good things might be done, objects of sentiment and a passing piety. ... but a certain amount of money had come to the people once known as Harijans, a certain amount of education, and with that then had also come the group sense and political consciousness. They had ceased to be abstractions. They had begun to do things for themselves. They had become people stressing their own particularity, just as better-off groups in India stressed their particularities.[4]

Naipaul's work deals with various sections of Indian society, who are struggling either for their lost rights, dignity or identity (in the case of the Dalits). According to him during the British rule, India had the Mutiny of 1857, but in the post-Independence era, he sees mutinies getting multiplied everywhere in India. According to him:

> Independence was worked for by people more or less at the

> top; the freedom it brought has worked its way down. People everywhere have ideas now of who they are and what they owe themselves... The liberation of spirit that has come to India could not come as release alone. In India, with its layer below layer of distress and cruelty, it had to come as a disturbance. It had to come as rage and revolt. India was now a country of a million little mutinies.[5]

So according to Naipaul this is true of Dalits today. "The liberation of the spirit" has touched them also. They today perhaps have felt for the first time deeply the inner pain "of distress and cruelty", which they have suffered for centuries. This pain has taken the form of "rage and revolt", which in a real sense has become the basis of their emergence as a political force.

Factors Responsible for the Emergence

The emergence of the Dalit movement as a political force has over a hundred years of history behind it. This history began with the establishment of British rule after the Mutiny of 1857 after which the political power of the East India Company was transferred to the English Crown. Almost at the same time was the beginning of mass conversion of the Dalits to the Christian faith. The establishment of British rule brought out the possibility of sharing in the decision-making process by different sections of Indian society including the Dalits.[6] On the other hand mass conversion and Christian missionary teaching brought the idea of equality among all. The mass conversions also brought awakening among followers of other faiths, particularly Hindus about themselves. S.K. Gupta says in this regard:

> The educated Hindus decried conversions and proselytizing activities of the Christian missionaries, but at the same time advocated reform... It was this modern spirit and form of the social revolt, emerging as a result of confrontation between the two cultures that augured well for the depressed class.[7]

But in this tussle of major religions in some parts of the

country, the Dalits opted even for their own separate religious identity, which later on contributed to their political identity also. The best examples of these are Ad Dharmi (followers of the original religion) and Adi Dravida (original inhabitants).[8]

The other factor which directly contributed to raising the consciousness of the Dalits is what historians call the "Politics of numbers". The British introduced Census in 1881 mainly for administrative purpose. According to them, Indians were not "one nation", but in fact "many", which were based upon various factors such as language, religion, race or even caste. The policy behind the census system in real truth was "the politics of numbers", because the census tells clearly where each community stands numerically and with the figures one can easily guess how much power or place one will have in a political system.[9] But the politics of number helped the Dalits more positively, because it helped in establishing their separate identity, about which Gupta says: "The depressed class (Dalits) themselves had become conscious of their political importance and wanted to maintain and assert their independent identity."[10] John Webster makes the same point clearer when he says: "The politics of numbers proved to be decisive in shaping not only the political identity and destiny of all Dalits, but also the future relationship between the Dalit movement and the Christian Church in India."[11]

There are a number of other factors and events which took place from the time of Ambedkar's entry into the struggle of the Dalits in 1919. Ambedkar's beginning, with his testimony before the Southborough Committee reached the climax of his struggle through his conversion to Buddhism on October 14, 1956 and with his idea of creating the Republican Party, and finally his death on December 6, 1956.

One other important factor, which has contributed to the revival of the Dalit movement in independent India, is also linked with Ambedkar; for it was during his birth centenary celebrations (birth April 14, 1891) and after, that much of the literature has come to light again. Already eleven volumes of his writings and speeches have been published by the Government of Maharashtra (Volumes 5 and 7 are directly concerned with the issues of Dalits and are used in this work). A number of other books about the Dalit movement have now appeared.[12] The works of Ambedkar and others have become the basis for the emergence of the Dalit movement.[13] What kind of force this Dalit emergence is politically will be discussed in the following pages to provide at least a partial answer.

Dalit Politics in Post-Independence Era

Political Parties

Prior to 1942 Dalits had no political party of their own. It was partly because Gandhi and the Congress were against the Dalits having an independent political party or identity of their own.[14] Therefore the founding of the All-India Scheduled Castes Federation (AISCF) in 1942 by B.R. Ambedkar was the first such attempt. Its aim of having a share in political power was stated clearly by Ambedkar himself in these words:

> I am definitely of the opinion that in this country political rights must be shared between the Hindus, the Mussalmans and the Depressed Classes. The Depressed Classes must by law have proper share in the government of the country along with the Hindus and Mussalmans. The future constitution can only work if it rests on these three pillars. To achieve this you must all come together under one flag and have only one organisation. If we have so far not achieved this position in the Constitution, which is due to us, it is because we have not united. If you all unite and work under one organisation, I have no doubt that you will reach the position you are entitled to.[15]

The object of the AISCF was:

> ... attainment by the Scheduled Castes of a status as a distinct and separate element in the national life of India and to obtain for them their political, economic and social rights to which they are entitled by reason of their needs, their numbers and their importance.[16]

Membership of AISCF was restricted to Scheduled Castes and the federation contested only the seats reserved for the Scheduled Castes. It had functioning branches in the Panjab, Uttar Pradesh, Bengal, Madras, and Central Provinces. It continued to function till 1956, when Ambedkar decided to disband AISCF and in its place was thinking of forming another organisation not restricted to the Scheduled Castes only. He wanted to call it "People's Democratic Party", but was persuaded to change the title so as not to sound "communistic". The word "people" was increasingly being used by the Marxists throughout the world. Therefore he chose to call his party Republican Party of India (RPI). He prepared the constitution and circulated it to the leaders of the Scheduled Castes and other minorities and backward classes. But unfortunately he died on December 6, 1956. The party as Republican was formally founded after his death on October 30, 1957 with the aim "to be the defender of the interests of the Dalit classes, the adivasis or tribal peoples, the backward classes, the Nava Bauddha society, the working classes, the peasant classes and the landless labourers."[17] The leaders and workers joined the newly formed party. Prominent among those who joined the All India Executive Committee were Rao Bahadur N. Shivaraj, Dada Saheb S.K. Gaekwad, B.D. Khobragade, popularly known as Barrister Khobragade. The RPI still under the old name the AISCF entered into electoral alliance with the Samyukata Maharashtra Samiti and succeeded in returning six members to the Lok Sabha and nineteen to the State Assembly.[18] It had considerable presence in the State Legislature at Uttar Pradesh, Madras and Madhya Pradesh.

RPI launched an agitation for redistribution of land besides other demands like implementation of reservation orders. RPI in Uttar Pradesh and Maharashtra, Madhya Pradesh and Panjab was a growing force. The strongest presence was in Maharashtra. Congress leaders, afraid of the growing strength of the Dalits' party, set about weakening it. D.T. Rupawate, Dada Saheb Gaekwad, R.D. Bhandare, B.C. Kamble, Haridas Awle, B.D. Khobragade were the prominent leaders. The then Chief Minister Y.B. Chavan befriended B.K. Gaekwad who was easily taken in. Jan Sangh was another upper caste-dominated party which was growing in strength. The Congress did not want the RPI to join hands with the opposition party. The Dalits did not believe the Communists, because they had never been friends of the Dalits. The class character of the leaders had much to do with it. The agitation launched by the RPI had widened and strengthened its base.

The RPI wanted extension of reservation to the converts to Buddhism. Secondly, they wanted the Deeksha Bhoomi to be allotted to a Buddhist organisation to construct a memorial. It was small price to pay and the Congress Government led by Y.B. Chavan easily accepted these. The RPI entered into an alliance with the Congress for the forthcoming elections and that had far- reaching repercussions. A split occurred. Some of the leaders justified the alliance on the plea that the Congress was liberal and more secular. Others thought, why stop at "alliance" why not join it. These leaders attached much importance to positions in the cabinet and presence in the Legislature. Owing to the expenditure involved and the election system they had no hope of joining the Legislature. D.T. Rupwate was the first to join the Congress. He was followed by another stalwart R.D. Bhandare. In the north, B.P. Maurya was the most prominent among the leaders of the RPI. He was elected on the RPI ticket in the first election. After the end of the first term he also joined the Congress. Rupwate was made minister. Bhandare was elected to Parliament and later on was appointed as Governor of Bihar. Maurya was also appointed as minister, but he had lost the trust of Muslim supporters and the Dalit followers and so met with electoral defeat.

Inevitably the party split. A faction led by R.G. Gawai who took over after the death of B.K. Gaekwad was pro-Congress. A faction led by B.D. Khobragade was supposed to be independent. Another faction led by B.G. Kamble operated in some parts of Maharashtra. Divisions never strengthen any party or group. Factionalism within a small party with little resources and restricted to some castes of the Dalits did enormous harm to the great work started by Ambedkar.[19]

Frustrated by these developments some young men chose writing and preparing literature. Like the angry Black writers of America they started through their writing depicting the horrible conditions in which the Dalits lived and worked and the atrocities committed against them in the villages. A militant movement on the pattern of the American writers and Black Panthers was started in Maharashtra. Dalit literature—poems and stories, novels etc., written by Dalit writers and poets—was recognised and commented on by the Hindu press and writers. Dalit panthers made angry speeches and when the seats in the areas having large populations of Dalits were given to Hindu candidates they launched an agitation calling on people to boycott the elections. The pressure tactics worked. They also visited in large numbers the villages where atrocities were committed by upper caste people.[20]

The Dalit Panthers were recognised as a new force in the politics of India. Panthers released a Manifesto, which indicated Marxist influence. Dhosal was one of the main leaders of the Dalits. Most of the Panthers owing allegiance to Ambedkar were against Communists. The Panthers got split and many had already been involved in criminal cases, because of the violent acts committed by them. The Panthers often criticised the RPI leaders for their intemperate habits, anti-Ambedkarite activities, going around with Congressmen and so on. Those involved in criminal cases individually approached Congress leaders for help and managed to get the cases withdrawn. Some were convicted.

Faction ridden, the RPI had ceased to have any voice. Its leaders entered into alliances with Congress and other parties and begged for some seats and money to contest elections. Several attempts were made by well-wishers of the party to bring about unity, but the unity did not last more than a few days.[21]

The All-India Samata Sainik Dal founded by B.R. Ambedkar was revived by Bhagwan Das and his colleagues in the Ambedkarite movement. Bhagwan Das had also founded Ambedkar Mission Society to promote the ideology of Ambedkar.[22] Bhagwan Das founded United Republican Party and contested elections in Delhi under its banner. This succeeded in bringing about unity among small factions, but failed to bring the major factions closer. New leaders emerged. Prakash Rao Ambedkar formed the Republican Party (Prakash) and tried to create a following. He is still working to create a strong base among the

Dalits, other backward classes and other religious minorities. But he lacks a strong party machinery and clear-cut ideology or programme to attract people.[23]

The Bahujan Samaj Party (BSP) was founded by Kanshi Ram in the late 1980s. He introduced himself to the Dalits by joining the Backwards, and Minority Communities Employees Federation. On the whole Kanshi Ram does not also have a clear-cut ideological basis, but still he rose as a prominent leader and floated his party, the Bahujan Samaj Party. During the 1985 elections the BSP could not win a single seat, but the party succeeded in returning two persons to Parliament in 1990 and with the alliance of backward class people it managed to return thirteen members to the Uttar Pradesh State Legislature. But in the November 1993 Assembly elections in Uttar Pradesh BSP won 69 seats and its ally Samajwadi Party (SP), a party of backward classes, won 107, and together BSP and SP formed the Government in Uttar Pradesh.[24] The BSP-SP success has been attributed to the Dalits and minority (Muslim) votes. "The SP-BSP combine also gained from the fact that there was an unusually large turnout of Dalit and Muslim voters. The strong Dalit presence was attributed to the magic of Kanshi Ram, and the strict security arrangements that allowed these people to exercise their franchise without fear."[25]

Dalits and Protests

Reference has been made at the beginning of this chapter to the mass conversion of the Dalits, which mostly took place during the last quarter of the ninrteenh century and during the first quarter of the twentieth century. A historian interprets this mass movement as the beginning of the modern Dalits movement.[26] But actually, the proof of this kind of protest or rejection of the past or rejection of a religious system, which continues to keep millions of people captive as non-human beings, was openly seen on October 14, 1956, when Ambedkar embraced Buddhism along with a large number of his followers. It was a protest of rejection of the oppressive socio-religious system completely.

The other example of such a protest is when 220 Hindu Dalit

families of a Tamil Nadu village, Meenakshipuram, on February 19, 1981 embraced Islam. Here the basic reason was the ongoing exploitation of the Dalits by caste Hindus and atrocities committed by the police. "Meenakshipuram Conversion", as this protest of the Dalits is known, received attention almost from all the political parties, including the Congress, Janata Dal, Bharatiya Janata Party, Republican Party of India and various regional parties of South India. Except the Republican Party of India, all others opposed the conversion.[27]

There are many other examples of such protests of the Dalits. The anti-Dalit riots of 1978 connected with the renaming of Marathwada University after Ambedkar was another well-known historical incident. When the State Government passed a resolution announcing the change of name, the upper caste opposition took this as a symbol of the Dalits emerging as a power. Hundreds of Dalits' houses were burnt and many Mahar Dalits lost their lives.[28] A Marathi Dalit poet, Mina Gajbhiye, expressed his anguish at anti-Dalit sentiment in one of his poems, which is translated as:

> I had sutured with difficulty the weeping wound of centuries
> Those stitches are all ripped out, ripped out by Marathwada
> Even our old bonds of give and take are snapped
> From now on I won't scream "I want to live"
> From now on I'll live to die
> Let the village become a burning ground with me
> I will not live like a dog, nowhere.[29]

Dalit Solidarity Programme

Historically, the efforts and work carried on during the last two decades by numerous Church-related and non-Church-related organisations, action groups and individuals are responsible for the formation of "Dalit Solidarity Programme", DSP for short. . . But basically it is a result of the awakening of the Dalits themselves to their solidarity, which was already there, but of which they were not aware.[30] DSP has not come into existence on the initiative of the World Council of Churches (WCC), as some people think. It is the Dalits who have helped WCC to reach a stage where it has opened its doors for receiving the guidelines and agenda from the Dalits, so that it may offer its enabling assistance to achieve the goals determined by the Dalits themselves. WCC's position became clear during its Seventh Assembly held in Canberra, Australia (February 7-20, 1991). In its statement on "Indigenous Peoples (Tribals) and Land Rights", it said: "We affirm the growing consciousness of Indigenous peoples' struggle for freedom, including those of the Dalits of India."[31]

After the above historic mandate, the department of the "Programme to Combat Racism" (PCR) of WCC approached representatives of various Dalit groups, who told the PCR that the Dalits themselves would prepare the agenda and would also let WCC know what are the areas in which they needed assistance from it. To prepare this agenda about 150 delegates representing different sections of the Dalits belonging to the various faiths (Christians, Buddhists, Hindus, Muslims and Sikhs) came for a National Convention in Nagpur (Central India), December 28-31, 1992. This was a unique historical event, the first time that Dalits, came together detaching themselves from their religious persuasions to prepare themselves to fight a common struggle against their common suffering and oppression, because they share the common heritage which they have named as "Dalit".

At the Nagpur Convention unitedly the Dalits prepared a fourfold agenda: *First,* to strengthen solidarity among the Dalits all over the country. To achieve this goal it was proposed to hold ongoing consultations in different regions with a view to acquainting the people with the programme and to create a network. *Second,* to extend full cooperation to the indigenous people to achieve their full rights as indigenous people in our country. As 1993 was the Year of the "World's Indigenous People" declared by the United Nations, the DSP would join hands with various organisations and groups working for the welfare and advancement of indigenous people during this special year. *Third,* to liberate the education system, which had been used as an instrument of oppression against the Dalits, indigenous people and women. The DSP would hold and arrange seminars, consultations, camps, exchange programmes, visits of youth and women. *Fourth,* to internationalise and create awareness among the members of the international community about the problems, discrimination, oppression and loss of human dignity of the Dalits.[32]

Christians/Churches and the Dalit Issue

Response of the Churches

The "Dalit Issue" has been known among Christians in some regions of India for more than two decades in some form, particularly in those areas where various studies concerning caste-class programmes were being carried on by the Christian Institute for the Study of Religion and Society (CISRS) since the early 1960s.[33] Before CISRS efforts the National YMCA also undertook some studies connected with some sections of the Dalits during the 1920s under their series on "The Religious Life of India". These studies included *The Chamars* by G.W. Briggs,[34] Wilbus S. Deming, *Without the Pale* (the Life Story of an Outcaste) by Margaret Sinclair Stevenson[35] and *The Mahar Folk* by Alexander Robertson.[36] In the middle of the 1970s, the Christian Institute of Religious Studies, Batala, also made some efforts to introduce issues related to the Christian Dalits by organising seminars and consultations in Northwest India on the theme "Self-Image of the Christians in Punjab".[37]

Officially, now the churches in India also have started responding to the Dalit issue. For example in the meetings of the Church of North India Synod October 6–10, 1992, the Synod unanimously decided to extend its full solidarity with the Dalits in general and Christians in particular by passing the following resolution:

> RESOLVED that on the basis of the Moderator's concern for Christians of Scheduled Castes Origin expressed in Section (9) of his Inaugural Address to this Synod and on the basis of Section (2) of the Report of the CNI Commission on Religion and Life regarding "Privileges for Dalit Christians", the

following concerns on Christian Dalits be noted and actions of solidarity with them be taken:

(i) *Recognition of the Problem:* The Synod of the CNI recognises the problem of Dalit Christians within the Church and outside it.

(ii) *Demand for Equal Rights:* The demand of the Christian Dalits for equal rights from the Government—that they be given the same rights and economic privileges and benefits as are given to Hindu Dalits and Buddhist Dalits—be supported and the Government be asked to make appropriate changes in the Presidential Order of 1950 to provide for equal rights and benefits to Christian Dalits.

(iii) The CNI Synod approve efforts for long-term planning and action for justice to Christian Dalits.

(iv) The CNI Synod authorise the Synod's Executive Committee, office-bearers, and the CNI Commission on Religion and Life to support the all-India movement for securing justice and equal rights for Christian Dalits.

(v) The CNI Synod authorise the Dioceses and Pastorates to support the cause of Christian Dalits, and the movement of Christian Dalits for justice morally and financially till justice is meted out to them.[38]

During 1992 the General Body meeting of the Catholic Bishops' Conference of India held at Pune, passed the following resolution with regard to the Dalit Issue:

> Doubtless among the more important and urgent problems facing the Church, we must mention the Dalit Movement specially in the South... We ask all to work unitedly to see that justice is meted out to our Dalit brethren.

The demands of the Dalits can be put mainly under three heads:

1. *Those which concern socio-economic benefits, education housing, jobs, etc.*
   The Church has done much in this regard. We have asked Regional and Diocesan authorities to redouble their efforts

on a priority basis with a special emphasis on education for all. National, Regional and Diocesan Social Service Societies will tackle this problem on a priority basis. Other dioceses of India within their possibilities, will be at their service.

2. *Empowerment of the Dalits in the structures of the Church.*
   This is an urgent request; only it takes time. Many efforts have been made and more needs to be done as soon as it is possible, without waiting to do the most perfect. We ask all to work patiently, unitedly and in Christian spirit towards this end. If this is achieved, we will have resolved an important aspect of this question.
3. *Respect.*
   This demands that Catholics of the upper castes—Bishops, Priests, Religious, Laity—change their attitude towards the Dalits. In the Church, all are God's children, our only glory being the sonship of God given to us at Baptism. "There is no distinction between Jew and Greek: all have the same Lord, who gives with abundance to whoever calls on Him" (Rom. 10, 12). We plead with all to reflect seriously on this, and by their change of attitude build up the Church of Christ, the one family of God.

   Our efforts in this line with the Government, must continue with unabated vigour. We urge all organisations at the national and regional level, which have been involved in them, to persevere and intensify their efforts.[39]

Along with the above efforts and challenges, already various networks, particularly the Christian Institute for the Study of Religion and Society (CISRS) are now conducting a major study in the whole area of the Dalit theology. The CISRS has divided the whole country into seven regions and various scholars and activists are working in each region on this project.[40] A number of other national and regional activists and action groups (such as Christian Dalit Liberation Movement)[41] are also making efforts at their own level, to deal with this issue locally and nationally. An "All India Christian People's Forum" has taken up the issue of the Christian Dalits' equal rights in a big way and is organising a number of rallies, both at the regional and national levels, to mobilise the grass-roots people to fight for their equal rights.[42] The National Council of Churches in India has also made the Dalit issue a part of their programme.[43] The Senate of Serampore College (University) and a number of its affiliated colleges have included the Dalit issue as part of their syllabus.[44]

Need for Building Political Action

It is clear from the discussion of Chapter One that because of physical defeat at the hands of members of the caste-structured society, members of the Dalit casteless community were forced to become serfs on the soil and menials of society through a systematic historical process. But it is not oppression which destroys people, it is the acceptance of oppression which destroys them.[45] The Dalits have lost their identity as human beings because they have accepted their inferior status assigned by members of the divided caste-structured society.

Any programme for changing this state of affairs should seek to raise the Dalits' consciousness to the reality about themselves: that they are remnants of a casteless community based upon a principle of equality;[46] and two, that their assigned inferior status is neither of their own creation nor a divinely created reality—it has in fact been imposed upon them by the humanly created caste system supported by both socio-religious and political actions of their opponents.[47] It is a long term objective for which all the Dalits belonging to various religious persuasions have to work. This is where the churches and Christians need to extend their support, because this includes political action in which Christians in India have been passive actors.[48]

But there are issues to which Christians/churches can respond. One such issue is the basic rights of Christian Dalits. This is directly related to the 1950 Presidential Order, which divided the Dalits on the basis of religion. This order has affected the bulk of Dalits belonging to different religions including Christian. Because of this Order, the Christian Dalits today have not only lost their basic rights as Indian citizens, but also have lost their fundamental human rights, as explained earlier.

As mentioned in the previous discussions, the Constitution has acknowledged the reality of the existence of certain sections in the Indian society, which are deprived and disadvantaged socially, economically and educationally. The Constitution calls them Scheduled Castes and Scheduled Tribes (Articles 15:4, 16:4, 46, etc.) But the Constitution has not stated who these sections of people are. It has only mentioned that these can be any men or women belonging to any caste, race or tribe. It does further empower the President of India (Article 341) to issue an Order identifying such sections of people who need special care and concessions for their development. In a way as far as the Constitution is concerned, one does not see any problem with this. But the real problem starts with the first order of the President, issued in 1950 concerning the Scheduled Castes for which he has used "religion" as a basis for the identification of such people.

This means Government will provide various kinds of aid only to those poor or under-privileged people who by religion are Hindus. This aid includes special facilities for education, economic aid and quota in government jobs. By keeping the Dalits out of the caste-divided society through the use of religion at one point of history they were declared "outcaste" or "Untouchable", but then the Indian Government has used the same means to control them by including them in the Hindu fold. This does not in any way mean that in 1950 they became part of the caste-divided society. In fact the Presidential Order has only given them an official status of the fifth caste with the title Scheduled Castes, by which now onward their old negative status of *panchama* (fifth caste) is confirmed legally by the Head of the country.

But the story of the1950 Presidential Order did not stop there. Not everybody accepted his order. The Sikh community struggled by using political means on behalf of the Sikh Dalits for rights, equal to the Hindu Dalits, and in 1956 Parliament amended the Order to include the Sikh Dalits along with the Hindus. Here one needs to remember that the President on the basis of Article 341 can only issue an Order as that of 1950, but he cannot amend it. The power to amend is given to Parliament alone. In 1990, Parliament on the occasion of the Ambedkar centenary celebrations, once again amended the 1950 Order and included in the list

Buddhist Dalits also. Christian and Muslim Dalits have still been kept out, because they have not raised their voice or made any efforts to fight for their rights.[49]

Here the basic problem of the Christian Dalits is that even after 1947 the Christian churches of India have not taken their side. The Christians of upper caste origin and those few Dalits who have somehow come up (in general), because of their vested interests have in fact opposed equal rights for the Christian Dalits.[50] But these two sections of Christians could have given leadership to the Christian Dalits, because without a leader nobody can start a struggle or movement, particularly of a political nature. It is here that the Christians of India are faced with a major challenge for response. A commendable attempt was made in this direction on August 17, 1990, when for the first time Christians and churches made a united effort through a rally in New Delhi, in which more than 100,000 Christian Dalits and others took part to demand equal rights. A Christian observer said that this rally had given Dalit Christians "new confidence in fighting for political rights. In addition, it gave them a new consciousness of themselves as Dalits as well as a sense of unity in addressing their backwardness in Church and society".[51] This process of building political consciousness has to continue among Christian Dalits.

Concluding Remarks

From the discussion in this chapter, the following four points become clear:

One, though the Dalit movement today indeed has emerged as a political force, the other existing political forces have made efforts either to weaken the Dalits' power or have tried to make use of them for their own benefit. *Two,* the Dalits in order to become a full political force have to work for wider solidarity among themselves. *Three,* Christians/churches should become facilitators with an enabling role, so that the Dalits may regain their lost dignity and humanity. *Four,* the Christians/churches need to enable Christian Dalits specially to organise political action in order to obtain their basic rights.

NOTES AND REFERENCES

1. Examples:
   a) Gupta, S.K.: *The Scheduled Castes in Modern Indian Politics, Their Emergence as a Political Power,* Delhi, 1985.
   (This is the best example of a work, which covers the period much prior to Independence, 1935-36 only).
   b) Lynch, Owen: *The Politics of Untouchability* (Chapter IV), New York (1969), pp. 66-128.
   (In the fourth chapter Lynch Owen discusses the political development of the involvement of a Dalit community of Uttar Pradesh *Jatav*, which includes pre- and post-Independence era).
   c) Gokhale, Jayashree: *From Concessions to Confrontation–The Politics of an Indian Untouchable Community,* Bombay, 1993.
   (This work deals with the political movement of the Mahars, a Dalit community of Maharashtra with special reference to B.R. Ambedkar's contribution and extensively with political developments in the post-Ambedkar era in the state).
2. Examples:
   a) A very good chapter on the post-Independence era is found in John C.B. Webster's work published in 1992 under the title *The Dalit Christians—A History* (Delhi). Webster discusses in detail the question of "Compensatory Discrimination", at the same time he uses all the basic materials concerning the Dalits issue from political perspective.
   b) Another very good example of an analysis of both pre- and post-Ambedkar era is a chapter on Dalit politics found in *Protest and Change—Studies in Social Movements* by T.K. Oommen, New Delhi, 1990, pp. 254-90.
3. *Times of India,* New Delhi, August 19, 1993, p. 6.
4. Naipaul, V.S.: *India—A Million Mutinies,* Calcutta, 1990, p. 4.
5. *Ibid.,* p. 517.
6. Gupta, S.K.: *op. cit.*, p. 146ff.
7. *Ibid.,* pp. 148-9.
8. (a) Robb, Peter (ed): *Dalit Movements and the Meanings of Labour in India,* Delhi, 1993, p. 285ff.
   Also see:
   (b) Kuber, W.N.: "Dalit Movements in India," in V.D. Divekar (ed.), *Social Reform Movements in India,* Bombay, 1991, pp. 101-3.
9. See for full discussion:
   (a) Gupta, S.K.: *op. cit.,* pp. 36-70.
   (b) Webster, John C.B.: *op. cit.,* pp. 76-8.
10. Gupta, S.K.: *op. cit.,* pp. 51-2.
11. Webster, John C.B.: *op. cit.,* p. 78.
12. Many of these titles are referred to in this work are listed in the bibliography also.

13. See for detailed discussion on 'Dalit Literature' in Gokhale, Jayashree: op. *cit.*, pp. 298-330.
14. *Ibid.*, pp. 120-4.
15. Das, Bhagwan (ed.): *Thus Spoke Ambedkar*, Volume III, Bangalore, n.d., p. 135.
16. *Ibid.*, p. 198.
17. Gokhale, Jayashree: *op. cit.*, pp. 217-8.
18. Zelliot, Eleanor: *From Untouchable to Dalit, Essays on Ambedkar Movement*, New Delhi, 1992, p. 114.
19. See for detailed discussion on the RPI formation, achievements, decline in Gokhale, Jayashree: *op. cit.*, pp. 212-55.
20. See for detailed treatment: Murugkar, Lata: *Dalit Panther Movement in Maharashtra*, Bombay, 1991.
21. *Ibid.*, p. 230.
22. See for references also: Juergensmeyer, Mark: *Religion as Social Vision*, Berkeley, 1982, p. 167.
23. In a personal conversion with the author of this work, Bhagwan Das shared these informations.
24. *Sunday*, 5-11 December 1993, Volume 20, issue 48, An Ananda Bazaar Publication, Calcutta, p. 37.
25. *Ibid.*, p. 39.
26. See for detailed information: Webster, John C.B.: *op. cit.*, pp. 33-76.
27. See for actual reactions of various political party leaders in: Khan, Mumtaz Ali: *Mass-Conversion of Meenakshipuram: A Sociological Enquiry*, Madras, 1983, pp. 3-7.
28. Webster, John C.B.: *op. cit.*, pp. 160.
29. Anand, Mulk Raj and Eleanor Zelliot (eds.): *An Anthology of Dalit Literature*, New Delhi, p. 77.
30. Beteille, Andre: *Society and Politics in India*, Delhi, 1992, p. 112.
31. PCR Information, Assembly 1991, No. 29, World Council of Churches, Geneva, 1991, p. 12.
32. See for detailed information: *The North India Churchman*, February 1993, XXIV/2, New Delhi, pp. 1-6.
33. Prabhakar, M.E. (ed.): *Towards á Dalit Theology*, Delhi, 1989, p. 20.
34. Briggs, Geo. W.: *The Chamars*, Calcutta, 1920.
35. Stevenson, Margaret Sinclair: *Without the Pale, The Life Story of An Outcaste*, Calcutta, 1930.
36. Robertson, Alexander: *The Mahar Folk*, Calcutta, 1938.
37. See for details: *Bulletin of the Christian Institute of Sikh Studies*, 6/I, January 1977, Batala, pp. 16-23.
38. Minutes of the 8th Ordinary Meeting of the Synod of the Church of North India, held at St. Stephen's College, Delhi from 6th to 10th October, 1992,

S:8:92-488(e), pp. 45, 46.

39. Quoted in "Dalit Christians: A Socio-Economic Survey", Archdiocese of Bangalore by Ambrose Pinto, S.J., Bangalore 1992, p. cover III.
40. XVI Biennial Council Meeting, Bombay March 12-15, 1990, Christian Institute for the Study of Religion and Society and Joint Programme, pp. 6-8.
41. See for the nature of CDLM activities:
    Struggles and Hopes of Christian Dalits in India: Perspectives for Ideology and Vision, Proceedings of the First National Consultation and the Second National Convention, Bangalore, Christian Dalit Liberation Movement, 1986.
42. See for details: the All India Christian Peoples Forum's Newsletter: *Network,* April, 1993.
43. National Council of Churches Review, CXIII/2, February 1993, p. 134.
44. Senate of Serampore College, Faculty of Theology, Syllabus, Bachelor of Divinity Degree, February, 1991, pp. 92, 215.
45. Cleage, Albert B.: *The Black Messiah,* New York, 1969, p. 20.
46. Wilson, Dr. K.: *The Twice Alienated–Culture of Dalit Christians,* Hyderabad, 1982, p. vi (Introduction).
47. *Report of the Backward Classes Commission,* First part (volumes I & II), Government of India, New Delhi, 1980, p. 14.
48. Ambedkar, Dr. Babasaheb: *Writings and Speeches,* Vol. 5, Education Department, Government of Maharashtra, Bombay, 1989, p. 472.
49. See for detailed discussion:
    Religion and Society, Vol. XXXVIII, 3, March 1991, Bangalore, pp. 26-36.
50. Shastri, Shankaranand: *My Memories and Experiences of Babsaheb Dr. B.R. Ambedkar,* Ghaziabad, 1989, p. 34.
51. Webster, John C.B.: "A Historic Rally for Dalit Christians", *Christian Century* (An Ecumenical Weekly), February 27, 1991, 108/7, Chicago, p. 238.

CHAPTER SIX

Need for a Dalit Theological Expression

(With a fresh understanding of Christian faith)

Introduction

It is clear from the discussion in Chapters Two, Four and Five that the Christians in India are divided into two main group: a large percentage, more than 70 per cent, are the Christian Dalits; the remaining 30 per cent include upper caste Christians and Christians belonging to various indigenous communities.[1] Another point made was that the religious understanding of the Christian faith or the theology of the early missionaries was and is partly responsible for the present state of the Christian Dalits. The successor to the missionary theology or the understanding of Christian faith, which mainly originated from the background and experiences of upper caste Christians, is also not quite relevant or effective in bringing about change, or in dealing with the problem of the Christian Dalits.[2]

Therefore there is need for another expression of theology, which will be relevant to the living situation of the vast majority of people in India, especially the Christian Dalits. During the last decade, a few collections of essays on the issue of the Christian Dalits have appeared either in the form of books or special issues of journals (either under the title theology or ideology), but these are not sufficient.[3] These works mostly make an analysis of the past and present situations, except A.P. Nirmal's one essay which has appeared with some revisions in at least four works under the title "Towards a Christian Dalit Theology".[4] In this essay Nirmal has very briefly dealt with the question of God, Christology and the Holy Spirit from a Dalit perspective.[5] A few other essays in collected works also speak about the need for a Dalit theology.[6] In this chapter the need for a Dalit theological expression is being reaffirmed, but more in relation to the historical background of the Christian Dalits (see discussion in Chapter Two) as well as of their basic rights (see Chapter Four). What are the basic requirements of such a theological expression? This discussion may be done under two heads:

(a) present Indian Christian theology and the need for a Dalit theology.

(b) requirements of a Dalit theological expression.

Present Indian Christian Theology and the Need for a Dalit Theology

Daliton ko swatantrata pradan karun (to let the oppressed go free)[7] said Jesus (Luke 4:18). At his first appearance in his village synagogue Jesus publicly announced his mission to the world, which included good news for *dinon* (poor), freedom for *bandion* (captives), sight for *andhon* (blind) and liberation for *daliton* (oppressed). This is what Luke recounts. So the concern here is one of the concerns of Jesus' whole mission. This now the mission of the Church, which includes every Christian, in India and elsewhere.

The question about theology is equally closely related both to the Church and the Dalits. After all, what is theology? According to M.M. Thomas, "Living theology is the manner in which a Church confesses its faith and establishes its historical existence in dialogue with its own environment."[8] Here the phrase which needs consideration is "own environment". Now what is the environment in which the Indian Church lives? It is a multi-faith or pluralistic environment. This is the reality to which till now Indian Christians and others, as thinkers and converts, have tried to respond. Certain responses to this reality have given birth to a theology currently known as "Indian Christian theology", which, however, is not really relevant to the living situations of the majority of the people. For, in simple terms, any theology is the local expression of the experiences of the local people of their faith. As mentioned earlier, the majority of Christians come from the Dalit background. It is these people's experiences which are missing from the present Indian Christian theology.

Looking at a standard textbook on Indian Christian theology,[9] one may say that the roots of the current Indian theological expression are in the experiences of mostly upper caste converts. Well known examples are: Brahmabandhab Upadhyaya, from a Bengali Brahman family,[10] Sadhu Sundar Singh from a high caste, wealthy Sikh Panjabi family,[11] Nehemiah Gore, a Marathi Brahman,[12] H.A. Krishna Pillai, a high caste Vaishnavite non-Brahman,[13] Narayan Vaman Tilak, from a Brahman family,[14] A.J. Appasamy, from a high caste Saivite family,[15] P. Chenchiah, son of a prominent upper caste lawyer from Andhra,[16] V. Chakkarai from the Chetty caste, a non-Brahman upper caste in Tamilnadu,[17] and so on.

If these names are deleted from current Indian Christian theology, there will be nothing left (see Appendix I). But the point which needs to be noted here is that these thinkers and their experiences and search were very different from those of an average Christian in India, because all of them came either from a high caste or their families were rich. After they became Christians, their immediate concerns were not the same as those of thousands of those who became Christians, who were both poor and belonged to the lower strata of society (mostly the Dalits). The high caste converts' immediate concern was how they should relate or interpret their new faith or experiences in Indian thought forms, that is based on the Brahmanic religion and culture in which they had grown.[18] Their major preoccupation was searching for an indigenous expression of Christianity, which forms an important element in Indian Christian theology. Arvind P. Nirmal has stated this point neatly in his essay in these words:

> To speak in terms of the traditional categories, Indian Christian theology, following the Brahmanic tradition, has trodden the *jnana marga,* the *bhakti marga,* and the *karma marga.* In Brahmabandhab Upadhyaya, we have a brilliant theologian who attempts a synthesis of Sankara's Advaita Vedanta and

> Christian theology. In Bishop A.J. Appasamy we had a *bhakti margi* theologian, who tried to synthesise Ramanuja's Vishistha Advaita with Christian theology. In M.M. Thomas we see a theologian... who laid the foundation for a more active theological involvement in India—the *karma marga.* In Chenchiah we find an attempt to synthesise Christian theology with Sri Aurobindo's 'Integral Yoga'.[19]

Thus the current or traditional Indian Christian theology, which is based upon the Brahmanic traditions of Hindu religions did not/ does not address itself to or reflect the issues which the majority of the Christians faced either before or after they became Christians. It is because this expression of theology is based upon the religious traditions of the minority even among the Hindu Brahmans (priestly caste) who represent only 5.22 of the total population of India. According to the Report of the Backward Classes Commission (1980), Government of India,[20] the percentage distribution of Indian population by caste and religious groups is as follows (see for details Appendix II):

a)	Scheduled Castes and Scheduled Tribes	22.56
b)	Non-Hindu religious Groups, Muslims, Christians, Sikhs, Buddhists and Jains	16.16
c)	Forward (upper) Hindu castes, Brahmans, Rajputs, Marathas, Jats, Vaishyas and others	17.58
d)	Remaining Hindus in the category of Other Backward Classes (Sudras)	43.70
	Total	100.00

From the above percentages representing different backgrounds which include religious, social and economic, it is clear that the current Indian Christian theology in a way has ignored the life experiences of more than 80 per cent of the Indian people, which includes the Christian Dalits (who form more than 70 per cent of the Indian Church). The majority of these Christian Dalits live in rural areas and are landless people. Their main livelihood is from working in the fields of others belonging to upper castes/classes. Therefore the Christian Dalits' concerns have not been to search for an Indian impression of their new faith. In fact, in this they are more indigenous than any of the urbanised Christians. What these village Christian Dalits have to search for is their daily bread, how to overcome their life situation of oppression, poverty, suffering, injustice, illiteracy, and denial of identity. The Indian Christian theology has failed them, and continues to ignore these issues, which for the majority of Christians and most other Indians are questions of survival. Here the main point is not rejection of the current expression of Indian Christian theology or its usefulness. All that is emphasised is that there is need to work out another expression of Indian Christian theology which would be relevant to the living situation of the vast majority of people of India, particularly the Dalits, based upon the living experiences of the Dalits themselves.

Requirements of a Dalit Theological Expression

There are three main requirements for the formation of a living form of theology: life context, history and language. Indirect references have already been made in the previous section to the first requirement, that is context.

The history of the people, the second requirement, is important for any theology. For Indian Christian theology, there is need of a history of the Indian Church or Christianity. Till now the Church history written in India is basically the history of western Christian missions; Indian Church history till now has been an appendage (in the words of M.M. Thomas) to this history.[21] The same has been true of Indian Christian theology. One of the first textbooks for theological students on Indian Christian theology, for example, was written by a missionary, with the subtitle "A Theology for India"; it is instruction-oriented.[22] It is as if missionary friends of Indian Christians still have to tell them what they need to do in their own context. Indian Christians have yet to write their own history from their own point of view (which has to be an independent story) and which will narrate how the Indian Church has confessed its faith and how it has established its historical existence in its own living situation. This reality has to be the basis of Indian theology.

The same is true of Dalit theological expression. This has to come out from the experiences of the Dalits themselves. It has to be based on the content of many living stories of the Dalits. It also means that the history of the Christian Dalits has to be prepared first.

The third important requirement is language. A report of the Commission of the Jesuits on "Formation and Inculturation in India Today" says: "For language, it is realised, is not merely the medium of expression or communication, it is, in fact, the vehicle of culture as a whole."[23] Many attempts have been made to write Indian Christian theology, mostly in English. But the Dalits here represent the concern of the masses; therefore, Dalit theologians have to use the language of the masses (of Dalits), in the formation of Dalit theology. This will be the most suitable way to maintain the originality of thought. To begin with there will be more than one expression of this theology, that is in Tamil, Bengali, Malayalam, Hindi, Punjabi, and so on. This will be according to the definition of a living theology, given above: "It is the local expression of the experiences of local people of their faith." To this may also be added that, to begin with, it has to be in the "local language".

Concluding Remarks

From the discussion of this chapter the following points become clear:

One, the present or traditional Indian Christian theology is the outcome of the experiences of the upper caste Christian converts, whose immediate purpose was to interpret their new faith (religious experience) in the light of their previous faith of Brahmanic Hindu traditions, which was, and is, a religion of a minority even within the Hindu traditions.

Two, because of the above reasons and others, the current Indian Christian theological expression is not relevant to the needs of the majority of the people, especially the Dalits, which also includes Christian Dalits.

Three, therefore there is need of another Indian theological expression, which has to be based upon the experience of the ordinary people, particularly the Dalits themselves, and these expressions ultimately will be according to the needs of the Dalits, which means it will become the basis of the struggle to regain their lost identity and basic rights.

NOTES AND REFERENCES

1. *Religion and Society* (CISRS), XXIV/3, September 1987, Bangalore, p. 49.
2. See for a brief discussion of this issue in:
   Nirmal, Arvind P.: *Heuristic Explorations*, Madras, 1990, pp. 139-43.
3. a) Works which have tried to deal with the question of theology:
   i. Prabhakar, M.E. (ed.).: *Towards a Dalit Theology,* Delhi, 1988.
   ii. Irudayaraj, Xavier (ed.): *Emerging Dalit Theology*, Madurai, 1990.
   iii. "Dalit Theology", *Journal of Dharma,* XVI/1, January-March 1991, Bangalore.
   b) Works which have tried to deal with the question of ideology:
   i. Nirmal, Arvind P.: *Towards a Common Dalit Ideology*, Madras, n.d.
   ii. "Dalit Ideology", *Religion and Society* (CISRS), XXXVII/3, September, 1990.
   c) Works which have dealt mainly with the history of the Dalits:
   i. "Christian Dalits and Caste in Churches", *Religion and Society* (CISRS), XXXIV/3, September, 1987.
   ii. Webster, John C.B.: *The Dalit Christians, A History*, Delhi, 1992.
   d) Works which make social and cultural analysis of the Dalit problem: the first one deals with the question of the Christian Dalit and the second one the case of women.
   a) Wilson: Dr. K.: *The Twice Alienated—Culture of Dalit Christians,* Hyderabad, 1982.
   b) Devasahayam, V. (ed.): *Dalits and Women,* Madras, 1993.
4. See:
   a) Nirmal, Arvind P.: *Heuristic Explorations*, *op. cit.*, pp. 138-56.
   b) Prabhakar, M.E. (ed.): *op. cit.,* pp. 64-82.
   c) Irudayaraj, Xavier (ed.): *Towards a Common Dalit Ideology, op. cit.*, pp. 123-42.
   d) Nirmal, Arvind P. (ed.): *op. cit.*, pp. 53-70.
5. Nirmal, Arvind P.: *op. cit.,* pp. 149-56.
6. a) Chatterji, Saral K.: "Why Dalit Theology", in M.E. Prabhakar (ed.), *op. cit.,* pp. 9-29.
   b) Clarke, Sundar: "Dalit Movement—Need for a Theology", *ibid.,* pp. 30-4.
7. a) *The New Testament* (Hindi), The Bible Society of India, Bangalore,

1967, p. 113.
b) *The Holy Bible, New Revised Standard Version*, World Bible Publishers, Iowa, 1989, p. 58 (New Testament).

8. Boyd, R.H.S.: *An Introduction to Indian Christian Theology*, Delhi, 1991 (Foreword).
9. *Ibid.*, pp. ix-xii (Contents).
10. Baago, Kaj: *Pioneers of Indigenous Christianity*, Madras, 1969, p. 26.
11. Andrews, C.F.: *Sadhu Sundar Singh*, Jullunder, 1970, p. 21.
12. Andrews, C.F.: *North India*, Oxford, 1908, p. 61.
13. Boyd, R.H.S.: *op. cit.*, p. 112.
14. *Ibid.*, p. 114.
15. Appasamy, A.J.: *The Gospel and India's Heritage*, London, 1942, p. 1.
16. Thangasamy, D.A.: *The Theology of Chenchiah*, Bangalore, 1966.
17. Boyd, R.H.S.: *op. cit.*, p. 165.
18. Job, G.V. & others: *Rethinking Christianity in India*, Madras, 1938, pp. 1-41.
19. Nirmal, Arvind P.: *Heuristic Explorations*, *op. cit.*, pp. 139-40.
20. *Report of the Backward Classes Commission*, First Part, Volume I & II, Government of India, New Delhi, 1980, p. 50.
21. Boyd, R.H.S.: *op. cit.*, p. i (Foreword).
22. Boyd, R.H.S.: *Kristadvaita, A Theology for India*, Madras, 1977.
23. Aixala, J.: *Jesuit Formation and Inculturation in India Today*, Anand, 1978, p. 21.

Summary and Conclusion

Summary

In the discussion in the six chapters of this work, the first thing that becomes clear is the power of the caste system supported by the ancient written scriptures of Hinduism and its role in creating the problem of the Dalits in India (see Chapter One). Besides affecting the Dalits' human aspect deeply, the power of the caste system becomes clear from the way this system influenced the other religions, which are supposed to be egalitarian in nature, which include Buddhism, Jainism, Islam, Judaism, Zoroastrianism, Sikhism, Lingayatism and Baha'i religion.

Even the most progressive egalitarian religion, Christianity, was contaminated by the caste system, as a result of which, it failed to deal with the problem of the Dalits in general and Christian Dalits in particular (see Chapter Two). The British rulers having a Christian background were not only forced to go in favour of the caste system, but also extended full official protection to it (see Chapter One).

In the post-Independence era again, the Indian national and state governments continued to perpetuate the old social system based upon the hierarchical *varna* system. At the same time, they tried to offer some ways and means to improve the condition of the Dalits. These efforts also failed, because these were and are limited to the various external symptoms of the Dalits' problem, instead of dealing with their psyche deep down , which has been conditioned by centuries of oppression and exploitation supported by both religious and political structures (see Chapter One).

The moment of history, from which the history of the present people known as "Dalits" began, was around the middle of the second millemmium. This conclusion is based upon the content study of the oldest literary source *Rigveda* and the findings of the archaeologists during the twentieth century. It has also become clear from our discussion in Chapter One that the Dalits are the descendants of the earliest inhabitants of India.

Chapter Two, affirmed that the problem of Christian Dalits is an existing reality. It was also discussed how the history of the missionaries both in South and North India right from the fifteenth century is responsible for the continuing problem of the Christian Dalits. Basically the missionaries' understanding of Christian religion of the medieval period (which included emphasis on other-worldliness, personal holiness, individual spirituality-based salvation, and so on), instead of helping the Christian Dalits to have the experience of full liberation, provided a way to escape from the realities of life, which entrenched them in their inner captivity. In the post-Independence era, the Christian Dalits have to suffer further on the basis of religion. For being Christian, they have not only lost their fundamental rights, but also their basic human rights (see Chapter Four).

The main point of the discussion in Chapter Three was the basic issue of identity, which the Dalits in India have lost. To regain that lost identity the Dalits have been making a number of efforts including change of religion. The recent awakening among the Dalits themselves has shown that they are keen to regain their basic rights, which are linked with the question of their self-identity.

Chapters Five and Six offer two possible strategies which can specially help the Christian community or the Church in India to take part directly in the process of regaining fuller humanity. Here political action based upon a fresh religious understanding is needed in order to strengthen the Dalits. If the Christians in India are interested in being in solidarity with the Dalits in general and the Christian Dalits in particular, they have to look for a fresh understanding of the Christian religion or faith. Here comes the need of Dalit theological expression (a political theology), which will enable the members of the Christian Church to take part directly in the struggle of the Dalits (see Chapter Six).

Conclusion

In conclusion it may be stated without doubt that if historically the Hindu religion through its caste system is responsible for the beginning and deepening of the problem of the Dalits in India, it is also true that other religions, both indigenous (Jainism, Buddhism, Sikhism, Lingayatism) as well as those which came from outside (Christianity, Islam, Judaism, Zoroastrianism and Baha'i religion) also were and are unable to fully help the Dalits in recovering their lost human identity, because these religions either could not save themselves from the powerful influence and impact of the caste system or could not face it.

An egalitarian religion like Christianity, if it has to enable the Dalits to recover their human identity, has to change its present form and free itself from the influence of the dominant religious culture (including the caste system) because that is not at all relevant to the need(s) of the Dalits. Instead it must move towards a fresh understanding of its faith based on the needs and experiences of ordinary people, particularly the Dalits, which will provide a possible way out for the Indian Christian community or the Indian Church to become an enabler of the recovery of the lost humanity and the basic rights of the Dalits in India.

Appendix I

Contents of the book

An Introduction to Indian Christian Theology by R.H.S. Boyd

Appendix II

Percentage Distribution of Indian Population by Caste and Religious Groups

S.N.	*Group Name*	*Percentage of total population*	
I.	Scheduled Castes and Scheuled Tribes		
A – 1	Scheduled Castes	15.05	
A – 2	Scheduled Tribes	7.51	
	Total of 'A'	**22.56**	
II.	Non-Hindu Communities, Religious Groups, etc.		
B – 1	Muslims (other than STs)	11.19	(0.02)*
B – 2	Christians (other than STs)	2.16	(0.44)
B – 3	Sikhs (other than SCs & STs)	1.67	(0.22)
B – 4	Budddhists (other than STs)	0.67	(0.03)
B – 5	Jains	0.47	
	Total of 'B'	**16.16**	
III.	Forward Hindu Castes & Communities		
C – 1	Brahmans (including Bhumihars)	5.52	
C – 2	Rajputs	3.90	
C – 3	Marathas	2.21	
C – 4	Jats	1.00	
C – 5	Vaishyas-Bania, etc.	1.88	
C – 6	Kayashtas	1.07	
C – 7	Other forward Hindu castes/groups	2.00	
	Total of 'C'	**17.58**	
	Total of' A', 'B' & 'C'	**56.30**	
IV.	Backward Hindu Castes & Communities		
D.	Remaining Hindu castes/groups which come in the category of "Other Backward Clases"	43.70[@]	
E.	52% of religious groups under Section B may also be treated as OBCs.	8.40	

F. The approximate derived population of Other Backward Classes including non-Hindu Communities 52%
(Aggregate of D & E, rounded).

@ This is a derived figure.
*Figures in brackets give the population of SC&ST among these non-Hindu communities.

Taken from:
Report of the *Backward Classes Commission* (Commonly known as *Mandal Commission*), First Part, Volumes I&II, Government of India, New Delhi, 1980, page 56.

Glossary

Arya	:	worthy, noble or high
Asura	:	a class of people in the *Rigveda* opposite to Arya
Adivasi	:	original inhabitant
Avarna	:	outside the fourfold caste system
Be-i-man	:	without religion
Brahman	:	priest
Brahmini	:	a female member of upper first caste Brahman
Brahman Sanyasi	:	Priest for the upper caste
Chaturvarnyam	:	four castes
Churha	:	an outcaste, by occupation sweeper
Chamar	:	leather worker
Chandal	:	Pejorative title given by the upper castes to the lowest caste
Dalit	:	broken or oppressed
Dasyu	:	or Dasa a name of opponent to Arya in the *Rigveda*
Deva	:	divine or god
Dhoti	:	unstitched cloth to wrap round the body
Hakimji	:	village physician
Huzoor	:	Sir
Han	:	Yes
Itihasa	:	history
Jat	:	farmer
Jamadar	:	Head sweeper
Ksatriya	:	Warrior
Karma	:	action or deeds
Lambardar	:	village head person
Lal Begi	:	an outcaste, by occupation sweeper
Mazhabi	:	a Sikh of scheduled caste origin

Madiga	:	In Andhra Pradesh name of a lower caste community
Masih	:	Christ
Nahin	:	No
Nisada	:	a title of an outcaste in Rigvedic literature
Ma-bap	:	literally mother-father
Pariaha	:	a member of a lower caste
Pandara Swami	:	Priest of the lower caste
Padree	:	Pastor
Pani	:	in *Rigveda* a name of a class or a community opposite to Arya
Panchama	:	Fifth (a title used for outcaste)
Quom	:	Nation
Raksasa	:	Literally demons (another class of people opposite to Arya in *Rigveda*)
Satru	:	Enemy
Saptat	:	Dragon (literally means seven)
Sapat Sindhu	:	Seven rivers
Sayyad	:	Prince
Shaik	:	Chief
Satyashodhak	:	Name of an organisation started by Jotiba Phule for the upliftment of lower castes
Swadeshi	:	Indigenous
Samaj	:	Community
Sahib	:	Master, lord, gentleman
Svarana	:	Clean caste
Varna	:	Colour or caste
Vaisya	:	Trader caste

Bibliography

PRIMARY SOURCES

a) Ancient writings, Translations and Old Publications:

Acharya Shriram Sharma (ed.): *Rigveda* (in Sanskrit with meaning in Hindi), four volumes, Sanskrit Sansthan, Bareilly (Uttar Pradesh), 1985.

Burnell, Arthur Coke (tr.): *The Ordinances of Manu,* New Delhi, 1971.

Goyandaka, Jayadyal (ed.): *Sukhipat Mahabhrate* (Hindi), Gorakhpur, n.d.

Griffith, Ralph T.H. (tr.): *The Hymns of the Rigveda,* Delhi, 1986, reprinted.

Hume, Robert Ernest (tr.): *The Thirteen Principal Upanishads,* London, Reprinted 1951.

Sen, Makhan Lal (tr.): *Ramayana,* Calcutta, 1989.

Swami Vireswaranda (tr.): *Srimad Bhagvad-Gita*, Madras, 1987.

The Holy Bible, New Revised Standard Version, World Bible Publishers, Iowa, USA, 1989.

The New Testament (Hindi), The Bible Society of India, Bangalore, 1967.

b) Earliest Publications by the Missionaries and Others

Anderson, William B. and Charles R. Watson: *Far North in India,* Philadelphia, 1909.

Andrews, C.F.: *North India,* Oxford, 1908.

Clark, The Revd. Robert: *A Brief Account of Thirty Years of Missionary work of the Church Missionary Society in Panjab and Sindh,* 1852-1882, Lahore, 1883.

Gordon, The Rev. Andrew: *Our India Mission,* 1855-1885, Philadelphia, 1888.

Kaye, John William: *Christianity in India: An Historical Narrative,* London, 1859.

Newton, John: *Historical Sketches of the Indian Missions of the Presbyterian Church* in *The United States of America,* Allahabad, 1886.

Possehl Gregory L. (ed.): *Ancient Cities of the Indus,* New Delhi, 1979. (Contains original essays written between 1924-1979).

Taylor, H.F. Lechmene: *In the Land of the Five Rivers, A sketch of the work of the Church of Scotland in the Panjab,* London, 1906.

c) Government Original Documents and Reports

Census of India, 1991, Series 1, India, Paper 1 of 1992, Final Population Totals, New Delhi, 1993.

"*Karnataka Backward Classes Commission* (Constituted under the Commissions of Inquiry Act, 1952), Report," Volume I, Part I, Bangalore, 1975.

Report of the Backward Classes Commission, First Part, Volume I & II, Government of India, New Delhi, 1980.

Report of the Commissioner for Scheduled Castes and Scheduled Tribes (April 1985-March 1986). Eighth Report, Government of India, New Delhi.

Scheduled Castes and Scheduled Tribes (Prevention of Atrocities) Act, 1989 and Protection of Civil Rights Act, 1955 and Protection of Civil Rights Rules, 1977 with short notes, Fourth Edition 1993, Eastern Book Company, Lucknow.

Shrikant, L.M.: *Report of the Commissioner for Scheduled Castes and Scheduled Tribes for the period ending 31st December, 1951.*

Singh, K.S.: The Scheduled Castes, *People of India,* National Series Volume II, Anthropological Survey of India, Delhi, 1993.

The Constitution of India (As modified up to 15th August, 1989): Government of India, Ministry of Law and Justice, New Delhi, 1989.

Dictionaries and Other Sources

Apte, Vaman Shivram: *The Practical Sanskrit-English Dictionary,* Delhi, 1989.

Macdonell, Arthur Anthony and Arthur Berriedall Keith: *Vedic Index of Names and Subjects*, Vol.I, London, 1912.

Williams, Sir M. Monier:*A Sanskrit-English Dictionary,* Delhi, 1988.

SECONDARY SOURCES

a) Books

Aggarwal, Partap Chand: *Halfway to Equality,* New Delhi, 1983.

Ahmad, Imtiaz: *Caste and Social Stratification among Muslims in India,* New Delhi, 1978.

Aixala, J.: *Jesuit Formation and Inculturation in India Today,* Anand, 1978.

Ambedkar, B.R.: *Dr. Babasaheb Ambedkar, Writings and Speeches,* edited by Vasant Moon, Government of Maharashtra, Bombay, Vol. 5 (1989) and Vol. 7 (1990).

Anand, Mulk Raj: *Untouchable,* Bangalore, 1935 (reprinted 1970).

—— and Eleanor Zelliot (eds.): *An Anthology of Dalit Literature (Poems)*, New Delhi, 1992.

Andrews, C.F.: *Sadhu Sundar Singh,* Jullundher, 1970.

Appasamy, A.J.: *The Gospel and India's Heritage,* London, 1942.

Azariah, M.: *The Un-Christian Side of the Indian Church (The Plight of the Untouchable Converts*), Bangalore, 1986.

Baago, Kaj: *Pioneers of Indigenous Christianity,* Madras, 1969.

Banks, Marcus: *Organizing Jainism in India and England,* Oxford, 1992.

Beteille, Andre: *Society and Politics in India,* Delhi, 1992.

Baxi, Upendra: *Political Justice, Legislative, Reservation for Scheduled Castes and Social Change* (Dr. Ambedkar Memorial Lectures-1978), University of Madras.

Bhattacharyya, Haridas (ed.): *The Cultural Heritage of India, Evaluation of Religio-Philosophic Culture in India,* Volume IV, *The Religions,* Calcutta, 1983.

Bhattacharyya, N.N.: *Ancient Indian History and Civilization, Trends an Perspectives,* New Delhi, 1988.

Birth, Cyril Bruce: *An Introduction to Indian Church History,* Madras, 1981.

Boyd, R.H.S.: *An Introduction to Indian Christian Theology,* Delhi, 1991.

——: *Kristadvaita, A Theology for India,* Madras, 1977.

Briggs, Geo. W.: *The Chamars,* Calcutta, 1920.

Chanda, Ramaprasad: The Indo-Aryan Races, *A Study of the Origin of Indo-Aryan People and Institutions,* Calcutta, 1969.

Chatterji, Suniti Kumar: *Indo-Aryan and Hindi*, Calcutta, 1969.

Chattopadhyaya, K.P.: *The Indian Culture Contacts and Migrations,* Calcutta, 1970.

Chaudhuri, Nirad C.: *The Continent of Circe*, Bombay, 1983 (reprint).

Cleage, Albert B.: *The Black Messiah,* New York, 1969.

Dangle, Arjun: *Poïsoned Bread* (Translations from Modern Marathi Dalit Literature), New Delhi, 1992.

Das, Bhagwan (ed.): *Thus Spoke Ambedkar,* Volume III, Bangalore, n.d.

——: *Human Rights and Constitutional Rights,* New Delhi, 1987.

Das, D.P.: *The Untouchable Story,* New Delhi, 1985.

Desika Char, S.V.: *Caste, Religion and Country,* New Delhi, 1993.

Devasahayaram, V. (ed.): *Dalits and Women,* Madras, 1993.

Dharmaraj, Jacob S.: *Colonialism and Christian Mission Postcolonial Reflections,* Delhi, 1993.

Divekar, V.D.: *Social Reform Movements in India*, Bombay, 1991.

Dumont, Louis: *Homo Hierarchicus, The Indian Caste System and its Implications,* Chicago, 1990.

Dutt, N.K.: *Origin and Growth of Caste in India,* Calcutta, 1986.

Elst, Koenraad: *Indigenous Indıans—Agastya to Ambedkar,* New Delhi, 1993.

Fernandes, Walter (ed.): *Inequalities, its Basis: Search for Solutions*, New Delhi, 1986.

Forrester, Duncan B.: *Caste and Christianity,* London, 1980.

Frederick and Margert: *People Movements in Panja,* Bombay,

1978.

Freeman, James M.: *Untouchable—An Indian Life History,* London, 1979.

Fuchs, Stephen: *The Aboriginal Tribes of India,* London, 1977.

——: *At the Bottom of Indian Society,* New Delhi, 1981.

Galanter, Marc: *Competing Equalities, Law and the Backward Classes in India,* Bombay, 1984.

Ghurye, G.S.: *Caste and Race in India,* Bombay, 1979.

Gokhale, Jayashree: *From Concessions to Confrontation, The Politics of an Indian Untouchable Community,* Bombay, 1993.

Gore, M.S.: *The Social Context of Ideology, Political and Social Thought,* New Delhi, 1993.

Grant, John Webster: *God's People in India,* Madras, 1965.

Grewal, J.S: *Guru Nanak in History,* Chandigarh, 1979 (reprint).

Gupta, Dipankar (ed.): *Social Stratification,* Delhi, 1993

Gupta, S.K.: *The Scheduled Castes in Modern Indian Politics, Their Emergence as a Political Power,* Delhi, 1985.

Heick, Otto W.: *A History of Christian Thought,* Volume II, Philadelphia, 1966.

Hugh Kennedy Trevaskis: *The Land of the Five Rivers,* Oxford, 1928.

Hutton, J.H.: *Caste in India,* Cambridge, 1946.

Irudayaraj, Xavier (ed.): *Emerging Dalit Theology,* Madurai, 1990.

Isaacs, Harold R.: *India's Ex-Untouchables,* Bombay, 1965.

Job, G.V. et al.: *Rethinking Christianity in India,* Madras, 1938.

Joshi, Barbara R. (ed.): *Untouchable! Voice of the Dalits Liberation Movement,* New Delhi, 1986.

Juergenesmeyer, Mark: *Religion as Social Vision—The Movement Against Untouchability in 20th Century Punjab,* Berkeley, 1982.

Kananaikil, Jose: *Scheduled Caste Converts in Search of Justice, Constitution (Scheduled Castes), Orders (Amendment) Bill, 1990.*

——: *Scheduled Castes in the Constituent Assembly,* New Delhi, 1982.

——: *Constitutional Provisions for the Scheduled Caste,* New Delhi, 1974.

Kapur Singh: *Pundreek* (Panjabi), Ambala, 1952.

Khan, Agha and Hussain Bin Talat (Co-chairman): *Indigenous Peoples, a Global Quest for Justice, a Report for the Independent Commission on International Humanitarian Issues,* London, 1987.

Khan, Mumtaz Ali: *Mass-Conversion of Meenakshipuram: A Sociological Enquiry,* Madras, 1983.

Khare, R.S.: *The Untouchables as Himself: Ideology, Identity, and Pragmatism among the Lucknow Chamars,* Cambridge, 1984.

Kosambi, D.D.: *The Culture and Civilisation of Ancient India in Historical Outline*, New Delhi, 1992.

——: *An Introduction to the study of Indian History,* Bombay, 1991.

Kulke, Eckehard: *The Parsees in India,* New Delhi, 1993.

Kulke, Hermann and Dietmar Rothermund: *A History of India,* New Delhi, 1991.

Kurundkar, Narhar: *Manusmriti—Contemporary Thoughts,* Bombay, 1993.

Lokhande, G.S.: *Bhimrao Ramji Ambedkar,* New Delhi, 1982.

Lynch, Owen: *The Politics of Untouchability*, New York, 1969.

Mackay, Ernest: *Early Indus Civilization,* (Second Edition Revised and Enlarged by Dorothy Mackay): Patna, 1989.

Majumdar, R.C. and A.D. Pusalkar (eds.): *The History and Culture of the India People, The Vedic Age*, London, 1951.

Mandelbaum, David G.: *Society in India,* Bombay, 1990.

Marenco, Ethne K.: *The Transformation of Sikh Society,* New Delhi, 1976.

Mathew, C.P. and M.M. Thomas: *The Indian Churches of Saint Thomas,* Delhi, 1967.

Mukherjee, Prabhati: *Beyond the Four Varnas, The Untouchables in India,* Delhi 1988.

Mullick, S. Bosu (ed.): *Cultural Chotanagpur, Unity in Diversity*, New Delhi, 1991.

Murgkar, Lata: *Dalit Panther Movement in Maharashtra,* Bombay, 1991.

Naipaul, V.S.: *India— A Million Mutinies,* Calcutta, 1990.

Narasu, P. Lakshmi: *The Essence of Buddhism,* Bombay, 1948.

Nehru, Jawaharlal: *The Discovery of India, London,* 1951.

Newbigin, Leslie: *The Other Side of 1984,* Geneva, 1984.

Nirmal, Arvind P.: *Heuristic Exploration,* Madras, 1990.

—— (ed.): *Towards a Common Dalit Ideology,* Madras, n.d.

O'Hanlon, Rosalind: *Caste, Conflict, and Ideology—Mahatma Jotirao Phule and Low Caste Protest in Nineteenth Century Western India,* Cambridge, 1985.

Oddie, G.A. (ed.): *Religion in South Asia-Religious Conversion and Revival Movements in South Asia in Medieval and Modern Times,* New Delhi, 1991.

——: *Social Protest in India,* New Delhi, 1978.

Oommen, T.K.: *Protest and Change, Studies in Social Movements,* New Delhi, 1990.

Ouwerkerk, Louise: *The Untouchables of India,* Oxford, 1945.

Patil, Sharad: *Dasa-Sudra Slavery,* Pune, 1991.

Paul, Rajaiah D.: *The Cross over India,* London.

Phule, Jyotirao Govindrao: "Slavery" in *Collected Works of Mahatma Jotirao Phule*, translated by Prof. P.G. Patil, Government of Maharashtra, Bombay, 1991.

Picket, J. Waskom: *Christian Mass Movements in India,* New York, 1933.

Prabhakar, M.E. (ed.).: *Towards a Dalit Theology,* Delhi, 1988.

Rajaram, Navaratna S.: *Aryan Invasion of India, The Myth and the Truth,* New Delhi, 1993.

Rajasekhriah, A.M.: *B.R. Ambedkar—The Quest for Social Justice,* New Delhi, 1989.

Rao, Kande Prasada: *Freedom of Religion for Harijans in India,* Ongole, 1990.

Rao, R. Sangeetha: *Caste System in India: Myth and Reality,* New Delhi, 1989.

Robb, Peter (ed): *Dalit Movements and the Meanings of Labour in India,* Delhi, 1993.

Robertson, Alexander: *The Mahar Folk,* Calcutta, 1938.

Sachau's, Dr. Edward C.: *Al-Biruni:* India (abridged edition of Dr. Edward C. Sachau's English Translation and edited by Qeyamuddin Ahmed, New Delhi, 1988.

Senn, Frank C. (ed.): 'Pietism': *Protestant Spiritual Traditions*, New York, 1986.

Sethna, K.D.: *The Problem of Aryan Origins—From an Indian Point of View*, 1992.

Sharma, Ram Sharan: *Sudras in Ancient India*, Delhi, 1990.

Shastri, Shankaranand: *My Memories and Experiences of Babasaheb Dr. B.R. Ambedkar and His contribution to Nation*, Ghaziabad, 1989.

Singh, K. Suresh (ed.): *The Tribal Situation in India*, Shimla, 1986.

—— (ed.): *The Scheduled Castes, People of India*, National Series Volume II, Anthropological Survey of India, Delhi, 1993.

Singh, Ram and Nancy (eds.): *The Sugar in the Milk—The Parsis in India*, Delhi, 1986.

Smith, George: *The Life of Alexander Duff*, London, 1881.

Smith, Vincent A: *The Oxford History of India*, Oxford, 1958.

Srivastava, Suresh Narain: *Harijans in Indian Society*, Aminabad, 1980.

Stevenson, Margaret Sinclair: *Without the Pale, The Life Story of an Outcaste*, Calcutta, 1930.

Swami Dharma Theertha: *History of Hindu Imperialism*, Madras, 1992.

Talagari, Shrikant G.: *Aryan Invasion Theory and Indian Nationalism*, New Delhi, 1993.

Thangasamy, D.A.: *The Theology of Chenchiah*, Bangalore, 1966.

Thapar, Romila: *From Lineage to State*, Bombay, 1990.

——: *Interpreting Early India*, Delhi, 1992.

Tyndale-Biscoe (of Kashmir): *An Autobiography*, London, 1946.

Vakil, A.K: *Gandhi-Ambedkar*, New Delhi, 1982.

Veeramani, K. and P.R. Kuppuswamy: *According to Law We Are still Shudras—But How?*, Madras, 1989, p.2.

Walker, F. Deaville: *William Carey, Missionary Pioneer and Statesman*, London, 1926.

Watson, Francis: *A Concise History of India*, Southampton. 1981 (reprint).

Webster, John C.B.: *The Christian Community and Change in Nineteenth Century North India*, Delhi, 1976.

——: *The Dalit Christians, A History,* Delhi, 1992.

Wheeler, Sir Mortimer: *The Cambridge History of India,* Supplementary Volume, 'The Indus Civilization', Cambridge, 1953.

Wilson, K.: *The Twice Alienated—Culture of Dalit Christians,* Hyderabad, 1982.

Zacharias, (Fr.): *An Outline of Hinduism,* Alwaye, 1956.

Zelliot, Eleanor: *From Untouchable to Dalit - Essays on Ambedkar Movement,* New Delhi, 1992.

b) Journals, Bulletins, Newspapers, Minutes and Others

A Socio-Economic Survey Archdiocese of Bangalore, Bangalore 1992.

Bulletin of the Christian Institute for Religious Studies, 20/1, January 1991, pp. 3-6.

Bulletin of the Christian Institute of Sikh Studies, 6/I, January 1977, Batala, pp. 16-23.

Christian Institute for the Study of Religion and Society Joint Programmes, *XVI Biennial Council Meeting,* Bombay, March 12-15, 1990.

——, *XVIII Biennial Council Meeting,* Hyderabad, January 22-24, 1992.

Defences of Mandal Commission: New Delhi's Elite's Battle for Status quo, A Collection of Articles, Views and News, Documentation by LEAS, Madras, n.d.

Indian Sociology (edited by Louis Dumont), 16/2. Paris, 1992.

Indian Express, New Delhi, August, 18, 1991, Vol., p.8.

——: Wednesday, June 13, 1990, p. 3, column 3.

——: Madras, December 2, 1992, p.9.

Journal of Dharma, XVI/1, January-March 1991.

National Council of Churches Review, CXIII/2, February 1993.

PCR Information, Assembly 1991, No. 29, World Council of Churches, Geneva, 1991.

Proceedings of the First National Consultation and the Second National Convention, Bangalore, Christian Dalit Liberation Movement, 1986.

Religion and Society (CISRS), XXIV/3, September 1987, Bangalore.
——: XXXVI/4, December 1989, Bangalore.
——: XXXVIII/3, March 1991, Bangalore.
——: Vol. XXXIV/3, Bangalore, September 1987.
——: XXXVII/3, September 1990.
Senate of Serampore College, Faculty of Theology, Syllabus, Bachelor of Divinity Degree, February, 1991, pp.92,215.
Sunday, 5-11, 20/48, December 1993, Calcutta, p. 37.
Survey of the Evangelistic work of the Panjab Mission of the Presbyterian Church in the U.S.A., 1929.
The Christian Century (An Ecumenical Weekly), February 27, 1991, Vol. 108, No. 7, Chicago.
The Church Missionary Review, LXVI/790, February 1915.
The Examiner, The Catholic News Review, August 10, 1991.
——: 143/3, January 18.
The North India Churchman, February 1993, XXIV/2, New Delhi, pp.1-6
The Times of India, New Delhi, August 19, 1993, p. 6.

Index